THE INDEPENDENT GUIDE TO SHANGHAI DISNEYLAND 2020

G. COSTA

Limit of Liability and Disclaimer of Warranty:
The publisher has used its best efforts in preparing this book, and the information provided herein is provided "as is." Independent Guides and the author make no representation or warranties concerning the accuracy or completeness of the contents of this book and expressly disclaims any implied warranties of merchantability or fitness for any particular purpose and shall in no event be liable for any loss of profit or any other damage, including but not limited to special, incidental, consequential, or other damages.

Please read all signs before entering attractions, as well as the terms and conditions of any companies used. Prices are approximate and do fluctuate.

Copyright Notice:
Contents copyright © 2012-2020 Independent Guides. All rights reserved. No part of this document or the related files may be reproduced or transmitted in any form, by any means (electronic, photocopying, recording, or otherwise) without the prior written permission of the publisher, unless it is for personal use. Some images and text are copyright © The Walt Disney Company and its affiliates and subsidiaries. This guide is not a The Walt Disney Company product, not is it endorsed by said company.

Contents

Chapter 1: Introduction to Shanghai Disney Resort   4

Chapter 2: Planning your trip   5

Chapter 3: China: Know Before You Go   6
Visas   6
Payments, Tipping and Currency   7
Theme Park Etiquette & Culture   7
The Language Barrier   8
Mobile Phones, Internet Access and Wi-Fi   8
Weather and Travel Patterns   9

Chapter 4: Getting to Shanghai Disney Resort   10
Shanghai Pudong Airport   10
Shanghai Hongqiao International Airport   11
From Downtown Shanghai   11

Chapter 5: Hotels   12
Shanghai Disneyland HoteL   14
Toy Story Hotel   15

Chapter 6: Tickets   16
Online Tickets   16
Annual Pass   17
Early Park Entry Pass Ticket   17

Chapter 7: Understanding the Parks   18
When to Visit   18
Shanghai Disney Resort App   19
On-Ride Photos   19
Package Pickup   19
Fastpass   20
Disney Premier Access   22
Photopass   23
Rider Switch   23
Single Rider   24
Early Park Entry   24
Disney Concierge Services   25
Disney Premier Tours   26
Wheelchair and Stroller Rentals   26
Lockers   26
Spend Less Time Waiting in Queue Lines   27
Doing Disney on a Budget   28
Meeting the Characters   29
Ride Height Requirements   30
Park Entertainment Rules and Etiquette   30

Chapter 8: Dining   31

Chapter 9: Shanghai Disneyland Park Guide — 32
Mickey Avenue — 34
Gardens of Imagination — 35
Disney Pixar Toy Story Land — 37
Tomorrowland — 38
Fantasyland — 40
Treasure Cove — 44
Adventure Isle — 46
Shanghai Disneyland Entertainment — 48

Chapter 10: Touring Plans — 50
1 Day Plan for Guests with Early Entry — 50
1 Day Plan for Guests without Early Entry — 52
2-Day Plan — 53

Chapter 11: Outside the Theme Park — 54
Disneytown — 54
Beauty and the Beast – The Musical — 54
Wishing Star Park — 55
Shanghai Village (Shopping Outlet) — 55

Chapter 12: Guests with Disabilities — 56
Disability Access Service (DAS) — 57

Chapter 13: Shanghai Disneyland for Disney Park Veterans — 58

Chapter 14: The Seasons & The Future — 62

A Special Thanks! — 65

Shanghai Disneyland Map — 66

Chapter One | Introduction

Introduction

The Shanghai Disney Resort and Shanghai Disneyland are the newest theme park projects at The Walt Disney Company.

Having opened in June 2016, just 4 years ago, the park has enjoyed great success and over 30 million guests have walked through the gates. It is already the 8th most visited theme park in the world.

The project was approved by the Chinese Government in 2009, and with a groundbreaking ceremony in 2011, the entire resort took just 5 years to construct. Disney described the theme park as "authentically Disney and distinctly Chinese".

The resort is made up of two on-site resort hotels, the Shanghai Disneyland theme park, Wishing Star Park, and Disneytown (free admission), with shopping and dining experiences that cover a range of tastes.

Shanghai Disney Resort is not just a theme park or a place to ride roller coasters. Guests can meet characters, watch shows and parades, make new friends and enjoy an ambiance that no other theme park resort in mainland China rivals. Thrill-seekers may not find the world's tallest and fastest rides at the resort, but the quality of the experiences offered is second to none.

2020 is a fantastic time to visit as the resort continues to innovate.

Shanghai Disney Resort is a place where dreams really do come true for guests every single day, and you are about to become one of them.

Chapter Two | Planning

Planning

Planning a trip to the Shanghai Disney Resort can be daunting. You have to think about transportation, accommodation, food, park tickets, spending money, etc. This section aims to get you prepared by following the steps below. All of these steps are further developed in the chapters that follow in this guide.

•**Decide how you want to get to the resort** – will you be flying in, driving, or taking a train? If you are using public transport, be sure to check what time you will arrive at the resort and when you will be leaving so that you can plan your days accordingly.

•**Decide whether you want to stay on-site or off-site.** Do you want the convenience of being near the magic? Or, do you want to stay elsewhere?

•**Study the theme park maps** at the back of this guide and the official park map at https://bit.ly/shangmaps. Combine the maps with the details in this book and decide which attractions and shows you want to visit. Circle the ones you want to visit on your map or write them down. Knowing roughly where the park attractions are is essential to making the most of your visit. You do not have to memorize the map, but looking at it in advance will save you valuable time once you arrive.

•**Park opening hours vary wildly** – the theme park varies its opening hours according to how busy it will be – the more people are expected to visit, the longer the park stays open. The latest hours are on Shanghai Disney Resort's website at https://bit.ly/shangcal. Here you can see the park hours for the next 3 months. Also, you can click on any date for a Times Guide that tells you when the parades and shows are taking place, as well as the locations and times the characters are set to appear – this is very useful to know in advance.

•As **Shanghai Disney Resort is open 365 days a year**, it does not set aside a time of the year to close and perform its maintenance as most other theme parks do. Instead, the resort temporarily closes rides, shows, attractions, and park areas for refurbishment throughout the year. This is done once a year per attraction, usually during periods of lower attendance to limit the impact on guests. Refurbishments are published several months in advance. If there is a particular attraction you want to experience, make sure to check out the refurbishment schedule as part of the calendar at https://bit.ly/shangcal.

• **If you are traveling from outside China**, be sure to bring plug adapters (and possibly power converters), as sockets in China may differ from your home country.

•**Make sure you get your Chinese Yuan in advance.** Do not rely on buying currency at the airport. We recommend getting a pre-paid currency card that you can top up or using a credit or debit card with a 0% currency conversion rate. It is always handy to have some yen in cash.

The Independent Guide to Shanghai Disneyland 2020 5

China: Know Before You Go

Visiting China and the Shanghai Disney Resort is an exciting experience, yet it can be a daunting prospect for many – particularly Westerners who may never have step foot in Asia before. This section aims to help dispel some of the worries that you may have about your visit.

Visa

Important: Please take this Visa section with a pinch of salt – regulations and rules are always changing, so be sure to check that this information is still current before you book your trip. Planning is key!

Generally speaking, if your only destination is China on this trip, then most visitors will need a visa to enter China, unless your country has a bilateral agreement for visa exemption. For clarity UK, USA and Australian citizens are not part of these agreements and will need either a visa or to use a transit visa as mentioned later.

Getting a visa for China involves a visit to the Visa Application Center, lots of paperwork and then the approval of your visa. This is quite a lot of work and a lengthy process.

Alternatively, citizens of 53 countries can take advantage of a special 144-hour Transit Visa Exemption instead. The Transit Visa Exemption means that you are flying from country number 1 to China and then onwards to country 3. Country 1 and country 3 must be different countries – essentially, China must be a stopover as part of a longer trip.

For the purposes of this, Hong Kong counts as a separate country - this means you could fly from the USA (for example) to Shanghai, spend up to 144 hours in the Shanghai area, then fly to Hong Kong. This is a good way to see two Disney theme parks in one go.

You will need to have proof of a confirmed seat on your departing flight from Shanghai, and simply get the 144-hour Transit Visa Exemption upon arrival in Shanghai. There will be a separate queue for this at immigration at the airport.

We recommend having printed copies of the departure flight, arrival flight and hotel reservation with you when at immigration. You will also need this at the time of check-in for your flight to China – we recommend being at the airport early as some check-in agents may not be familiar with this Visa Waiver and think you need a visa.

As with all countries, you should note that entry to China under a Transit Visa Exemption or even a visa is not guaranteed - Chinese border officials have the right to refuse entry without warning or explanation upon your arrival.

You may see references to a 72-hour visa as well, but Shanghai is one of a few locations that has the longer 144-hour transit period for this exemption.

We recommend you contact the Chinese embassy in your country if you need more clarification. The British Chinese visa website has a detailed description of these schemes, but these details may differ from your home country - https://bit.ly/britchinvisa.

Payments, Tipping and Currency

China uses the Chinese Yuan as its unit of currency. This is abbreviated to either RMB or CNY, the symbol is ¥. At the time of writing, ¥1,000 is approximately $14.08 US, £11.37 GBP, or €12.75 EUR. Therefore €1 = ¥7.84, £1 = ¥8.79 and $1 = ¥7.10.

China has a wide variety of payment methods open to visitors – cash is accepted everywhere, and credit and debit cards (mainly UnionPay, Visa and Mastercard, and in rare places American Express) are widely accepted in cities.

Extremely popular are mobile payment apps such as WeChat (essentially China's Facebook on steroids with a chat app and payment system in one) – however, you won't need these as a tourist as cash and credit/debit cards will work fine everywhere.

The Shanghai Disney Resort accepts both cash and credit/debit cards at all Table Service and Quick Service restaurants, as well as shops. You will use a mix of both swiping cards without the need for a PIN (you must have a signature on the back of your card), and Chip and Pin.

In China, cards use six-digit PINs instead of the 4-digit pins used in the USA and Europe. Some ATMs will accept four-digit PINs, but for others you will need to two zeros before your PIN. Sadly, this doesn't work at all ATMs so check with your bank before you depart.

As for tipping, in restaurants 10-15% may be added to your bill as a service charge; you do not need to tip on top of this. If there is no service charge on the bill, tipping is not expected except at high-end establishments. In taxis, there is no need to tip, and we have had this refused on multiple occasions – if you do not have change, however, the driver may try to keep the rest as a tip. At Disney's hotels, the bell hops also refused tips on each occasion.

Chinese Theme Park Etiquette & Behavior

Visiting China is unlike a visit to any other culture, and visitors should be aware that a visit to a Disney theme park here will differ from that in other countries.

In terms of theme park etiquette, expect guests at Shanghai Disneyland to not have the same concept of 'personal space' as in the West. Particularly around characters, in queue lines, and during parades which can become quite pushy. Expect to see queue jumping, as well as a lot of umbrellas blocking your view of shows and parades.

Cast Members do not ask guests to stop standing on trash cans or waving selfie sticks during parades, despite both of these being forbidden.

It appears that guest behavior has improved since the opening of the park, perhaps thanks to Disney tightening its security, but previous reports include guests urinating in public, pushing in queue lines, shows and parades, leaving trash everywhere, selling fake Fastpass tickets and merchandise in the park, smoking, entering restricted areas and more. In 2018, a group of guests swarmed a Cast Member and stole the balloons he was selling.

We have not encountered any of this during our visits apart from the pushing during parades and the lack of personal space.

China has implemented a Social Credit system whereby good behavior is rewarded and bad behavior (such as crossing the road on a red pedestrian light) leads to a lower score. This can lead to not being able to even buy a train ticket or having permission to leave the country – with 1.4 billion people in the country, a small percentage causing a problem can lead to a huge mess.

The vast majority of the guests at Shanghai Disneyland are polite and follow the rules. Things seem to have improved and Shanghai Disney Resort has even launched a 'Star Guest' program with Disney characters used to remind everyone to follow the rules.

The Language Barrier

Although English education is a big part of China's school curriculum, many shy Chinese people struggle to master English, and also do not get the chance to practice it. Once you leave the tourist destinations, people are less confident in their English-speaking ability, and older members of society will likely not speak any English. Surprisingly, we find the level of English in Shanghai to be better than at Shanghai Disney Resort.

Visitors to Shanghai Disney Resort do have it a bit easier than in other parts of China – all signs and food menus are both in Chinese and English. Many shows have a mix of Chinese and English – songs are usually in English with the show script in Mandarin. The stories are generally easy enough to follow, even without understanding the language.

In our experience, the majority of the Cast Members speak very little (or no) English, but will try to help where possible. We found the level of English at concierge and hotel check-in, and at Guest Relations in the theme parks, to be the best with many staff speaking fluent English – in the rest of the theme park, we have sometimes struggled to even get directions to the nearest toilet. The Cast Members seem to know 'Hello', 'Yes', 'No', 'Bye, Bye' and 'Have a magical day!', but very little else, so a translation app can come in excellent use!

However, the Cast Members will go above and beyond to find someone to help you! We have even been escorted to another store across Mickey Avenue to find someone who spoke English to help!

The Shanghai Subway system is well signposted in English, with next stop announcements made in both Mandarin and English.

If you visit remote locations in China, English is likely not to be spoken at all.

Mobile Phones, Internet Access and Wi-Fi

Roaming
Your first option to use your phone in China is to use roaming on the SIM card that you use at home, if it is enabled. However, this is often exorbitant – check with your provider for pricing; some offer this service for a low daily or monthly fee, others charge hugely expensive rates.

SIM Card
Buying a local sim card can be complicated, so it is better to get one designed for foreign travelers. The solution is to pre-order a SIM card before arrival in China and then pickup when you arrive at Shanghai Pudong Airport. This SIM card will allow you to use data and calls while in China. Pricing is about £15/ €17/$18/¥2,500, including tax for a 10GB data card valid for 15 days (a 20GB version is also available). There are many other services available.

Look at Klook to see which option works best for you. This website is a one-stop-shop for entertainment and tickets in Asia. The above sim card can be purchased at https://bit.ly/chinasim.

Get an exclusive ¥40 discount on your first booking by signing up with this link - bit.ly/klookref.

E-SIM
If you are more digitally-minded and have a modern smartphone, then try an E-SIM instead which is a virtual sim card that is added to your phone. This means you still keep your normal sim card and phone number to receive phone calls and texts but use a virtual sim card for data. It is as simple as paying for your E-sim and then scanning a QR code on your phone – there is no need to order a card and then physically pick it up on arrival. Check Airalo – bit.ly/gotoairalo – plans vary with current offers such as 1GB for $7, 3GB for $14 and 5GB for $21 with operator Chicacom. Alternatively, China Unicom offers 5 days of unlimited data for $15.

As of February 2020, the compatible devices are iPhone XR and later, Samsung Galaxy S20/S20+/S20 Ultra/Z Flip/Fold, Nuu Mobile X5, Google Pixel 3/3XL/4/4XL/3a/3a

XL, Lenovo Yoga 630, HP Spectre Folio, iPad Air and Pro (3rd Gen), iPad Mini (5th Gen), Gemini PDA, and Motorola Razr 2019.

Wi-Fi Rental
There are also Wi-Fi hotspot rental services such as Uroaming at the airports. You can book this at Klook at bit.ly/chinawifi2 from ¥31 per day per device.

Internet access in China
The internet in China is censored by the government, so many websites and apps you may use daily such as Facebook, Uber and Google will not work in China as these are blocked by a firewall. WhatsApp is not banned at the moment. Many people use a VPN (Virtual Private Network) to get around this.

Free, fast (and censored) Wi-Fi access is available at Shanghai Disneyland like it is at the American theme parks. If you are planning on only using the Disney app to check wait times, for example, you will have no problem with the Wi-Fi.

The Disney hotels also have free Wi-Fi access, and free public Wi-Fi is common throughout China – Starbucks and McDonalds are always good bets if you see them. The Shanghai Metro subway stations also have free Wi-Fi.

Overall, we suggest having data access in China for translation and navigation. If you are only staying at Shanghai Disney Resort, you can probably survive on the free Wi-Fi only.

Weather and Travel Patterns

Spring
Spring temperatures range from 5°C to 24°C (41°F to 75°F) during the day. Apart from occasional showers, the weather is generally good. This is our favorite time of the year to visit – avoid the Labor Day Holiday around 1st May.

Summer
Summer is humid, particularly during June and July, when Shanghai's rainy season takes place. From late August to mid-September you can also expect typhoons with heavy rain.

It is worth investing in a good umbrella as raincoats are uncomfortable in Shanghai's summer heat. Summer temperatures range from 20°C to 32°C (68°F to 90°F) during the day, but the humidity means that the actual temperature feels higher. Make sure to stay hydrated and keep cool.

Fall/Autumn
Autumn is when the bulk of China's national school holidays take place, so family orientated attractions (such as the Shanghai Disney Resort) are extremely crowded during this time. You should particularly seek to avoid Golden Week, a string of national holidays for the first week of October – it is an incredibly popular time for Chinese people to travel and when over 1 billion people have the same time off, it can get very busy at attractions.

Temperatures range from 9°C to 27°C (48°F to 81°F). Outside of Golden Week, this is an excellent time to travel.

Winter
Snow in Shanghai is relatively rare, but the humidity makes bitterly cold days particularly unpleasant in the city. The New Year period is busy but in contrast to Western customs, Christmas is not celebrated as China's Christian population is only about 1%.

Daytime temperatures range from 0°C to 11°C (32°F to 52°F), with the end of January and February being the coldest part of this period. The winter months are statistically the driest months of the year.

Weather Averages by Month - First in Celcius, then in Fahrenheit in brackets

Month	°C (°F)	Month	°C (°F)	Month	°C (°F)
January	0-8 (32-46)	May	16-24 (61-75)	September	20-27 (68-81)
February	2-9 (36-48)	June	20-27 (68-81)	October	15-22 (59-72)
March	5-13 (41-55)	July	25-32 (77-90)	November	9-17 (48-63)
April	11-19 (52-66)	August	25-32 (77-90)	December	2-11 (36-52)

Chapter Four | Getting There

Getting to Shanghai Disney

By far, the most convenient way for international visitors to arrive in Shanghai (and access Shanghai Disney Resort) is by plane.

Shanghai is connected to the world by its two International Airports. Upon arrival in Shanghai, visitors must endure a strict immigration process that includes a fingerprint check; this can lead to long queues at immigration. Once through, you have the option of public transport or taxis to reach Shanghai Disney Resort.

In this section, we also cover access to Shanghai Disney Resort from the city of Shanghai itself.

Shanghai Pudong Airport

Shanghai Pudong Airport is the newer of Shanghai's two airports, and has the majority of international flights. The airport is connected to Shanghai via the world's fastest train – Shanghai Maglev Train, the subway, airport buses and taxis. To reach Shanghai Disney Resort there are also a couple of options.

Metro

Both Shanghai Pudong Airport and Shanghai Disney Resort are connected by the metro system. Unfortunately, they are not on the same line and therefore your journey involves changing lines twice to get to Disney.

You will need to take Line 2 (lime green) from the airport to Longyang Road (11 stops), and then transfer to Line 16 (light blue) for 2 stops to Luoshan Road, then transfer to Line 11 (brown) to Disney Resort – this is 3 stops. This journey will take around 1 hour and 20 minutes.

Then, once at the Disney Resort you will need to walk to the bus station (about 10 minutes) and catch the free hotel shuttle bus to either hotel, or the boat to the Shanghai Disneyland Hotel. This means the journey will take around 1 hour 45 minutes in total realistically. The fare is a bargain at about ¥9 (about $1 US).

Taxi

The other alternative is to take a taxi. This will take only 20 to 30 minutes and costs about ¥80 to ¥110. This is about 10 times the price of the metro, but it is door to door directly to your hotel, more convenient with luggage and as taxi rides go this is pretty affordable for Westerners.

Make sure to have the address in Chinese characters to show the driver and dispatcher – you catch the taxi on arrival from an organized queuing system just outside the airport terminal.

Shanghai Hongqiao International Airport

Shanghai Hongqiao International Airport is the older of Shanghai's two airports, and caters mostly to national and regional flights. The airport is connected to Shanghai via the subway, airport buses and taxis. To reach Shanghai Disney Resort there are also a couple of options.

Metro
Both Shanghai Pudong Airport and Shanghai Disney Resort are connected by the metro system. Unfortunately, they are not on the same line and therefore your journey involves changing lines twice to get to Disney.

You will need to take Line 10 (lilac) from the airport to Jiaotong University (7 stops), and then transfer to Line 11 (brown) to Disney Resort – this is 14 stops. This journey will take around 1 hour and 10 minutes.

Then, once at the Disney Resort you will need to walk to the bus station (about 10 minutes) and catch the free hotel shuttle bus to either hotel, or the boat to the Shanghai Disneyland Hotel. This means the journey will take around 1 hour 45 minutes in total realistically. The fare is a bargain at about ¥9 (about $1 US).

Taxi
The other alternative is to take a taxi. This will take 50 to 60 minutes and costs about ¥140 to 180. This is much more expensive than the metro, but it is door to door directly to your hotel, more convenient with luggage and as taxi rides go this is pretty affordable for Westerners.

Make sure to have the address in Chinese characters to show the driver and dispatcher – you catch the taxi on arrival from an organized queuing system just outside the airport terminal.

From Downtown Shanghai

The metro system allows you to go from downtown Shanghai to Disney Resort in about 40-60 minutes depending on your start location in the city.

The typical cost is around ¥9. You may wish to consider a day pass which costs just ¥18 and is valid on all metro lines in the city, or ¥45 for 3 days.

A taxi from downtown Shanghai to Disney will take a similar amount of time and cost around ¥100.

Chapter Five | Hotels

Hotels

Shanghai Disney Resort is only 4 years old in 2020, and when building the resort, it was estimated that most guests would only visit the theme park for one day.

Therefore, there are only two on-site hotels available – the more affordable *Toy Story Hotel*, and the more luxurious *Shanghai Disneyland Hotel*.

As well as the proximity to the theme park, the main benefits of booking a Disney hotel are:
● Stay close to the action – you can walk from both hotels to the theme park, or catch the shuttle bus (or water taxi for Shanghai Disneyland Hotel only)
● Disney theming inside the hotels
● Disney character dining at Lumiére's Kitchen in Shanghai Disneyland Hotel.
●Family Playrooms
● 30 Minutes Early theme park entry
● Priority seating at some restaurants
● Friendly and knowledgeable Disney Cast Members at the hotel
● Package delivery from the park to your hotel

Plus, if you book your hotel and park tickets as part of a package (or at the hotel), you can choose one Fastpass at check-in per person for each night of your stay. Booking the park tickets online separately does not entitle you to this benefit, as we found out much to our annoyance. Check this before booking as the offer may change.

We recommend booking your Disney hotel directly at shanghaidisneyresort.com – you can book hotels up to 6 months in advance.

Other Hotels

There are some hotels located near Shanghai Disney Resort, but there are no partner hotels like at other Disney theme park resorts.

The *Courtyard by Marriott Shanghai International Tourism and Resorts Zone* is about 3 miles from the resort. Then is also a *Novotel Shanghai Clover Hotel* about 5 miles away, and the *Holiday Inn Express Shanghai Kangqiao* around 6 miles away. To book these visit a hotel booking aggregator such as www.hotels.com.

For comparison, the prices included in this section are based on 2 adults sharing a room. For the same dates, the Holiday Inn Express was ¥485 to ¥500 per night, the Marriot was around ¥510 and the Novotel was around ¥630. All have free shuttle buses to Disneyland, and some even have free airport and downtown shuttles.

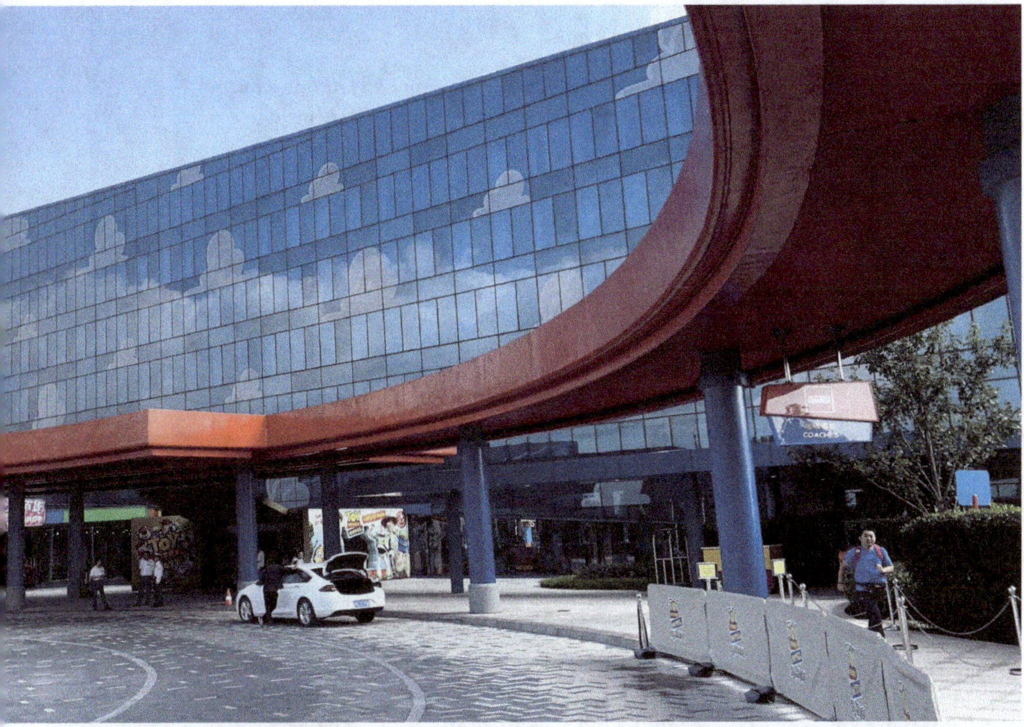

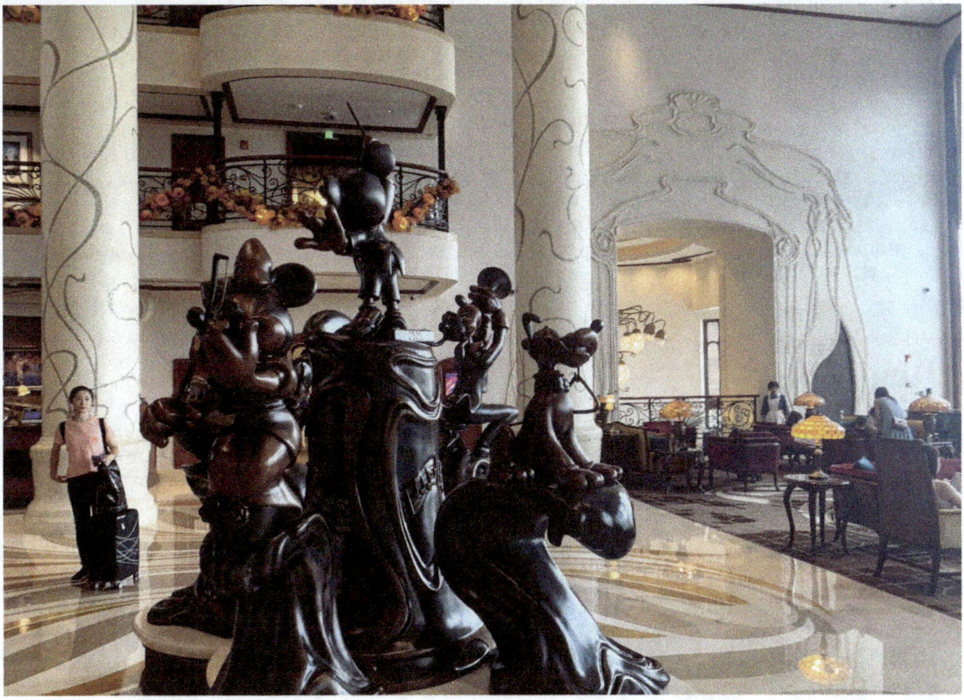

Hotels

Shanghai Disneyland Hotel

This 400-room Deluxe hotel is Shanghai Disney Resort's flagship hotel. It has an art deco theme and is the height of luxury. Enjoy staying just moments away from Shanghai Disneyland.

The Shanghai Disneyland Hotel is the most luxurious place to stay on-site. It is located across Wishing Star Lake from the theme park. This means you can wake up to the sight of the Enchanted Storybook Castle, and go to sleep seeing the fireworks from your window. This is the more 'grown up' of the two on-site hotels, but that doesn't mean it won't be fun for kids – this is Disney, after all!

The hotel features an indoor pool, a small 'gym' (just a treadmill and cycle machine), an outdoor water play area and hedge maze, character meets, live music in the lobby and a kids play center. There is, of course, an on-site Disney merchandise shop.

To reach the theme park there is the option of walking, a shuttle bus or a boat – all options take about 15 minutes to the theme park main entrance.
Breakfast: Not included.

Room Prices: (all prices include a 15% service charge not displayed when initially booking through the Disney website)
● Deluxe Garden View – ¥2,921 to ¥4,312 per night.
● Club Level Room – ¥5,292 to ¥5,405 per night.
● Magic Kingdom Junior Suite – ¥7,302 per night.
● Fantasia Suite – ¥11,902 per night.
● Sorcerer Suite (sleeps up to 6 adults) – ¥18,803 per night.

Extras: Complimentary Wi-Fi, ATM, luggage storage at bell desk, business center services, currency exchange, dry cleaning and laundry, mail service, package shipping, package pickup, and club level lounge.

Dining
Aurora – Signature Table Service dining experience with world cuisine. Amazing views of the park's castle. Entrees include Boston lobster, beef wellington, salmon, scallops, duck, chicken breast and more. This restaurant is offering a 'Kids Eat Free' promotion until 30th December 2020. Expect to spend around ¥1,300 for a set meal here, or at least ¥500 per entrée a la carte.
Bacchus Lounge – Lounge with lunch sets serving Chinese and Western cuisine.
Ballet Café – Snacks and Quick Service options. Offers breakfast set menus, and a la carte Quick Service dishes after 11am such as pizza, pasta and wonton soup.
Lumières Kitchen – Buffet dining with Disney characters with both Western and Chinese options. Expect to pay around ¥350 per adult (¥500 with alcoholic drinks) and ¥250 per child. This restaurant is offering a 'Kids Eat Free' promotion until 30th December 2020.

Toy Story Hotel

This 800-room Value level hotel is the cheapest on-site option at Disney and provides guests with the chance to stay in the Disney magic surrounded by their favorite friends from the Toy Story movies. This is a more affordable option to stay on-site and is around half the price of the Shanghai Disneyland Hotel.

The hotel is just across the road from Shanghai Disneyland meaning you can walk to the theme park in about 10 minutes, or catch a shuttle bus and be there in about 5 minutes.

The hotel does not have a pool, Table Service restaurant or gym, but it does have a water play area, and a play center. There are also character meets with Toy Story characters such as Woody and Jessie, and a Disney shop.

Breakfast: Not included.

Room Prices: (all prices include a 15% service charge not displayed when initially booking through the Disney website)
● Garden View Standard Room – ¥1,543 to ¥2,365 per night
● Courtyard View Standard Room – ¥1,854 to ¥2,370 per night.
● Park View Standard Room – ¥1,994 to ¥3,003 per night.

Extras: Complimentary Wi-Fi, ATM, luggage storage at

bell desk, currency exchange, dry cleaning and laundry, mail service,

package shipping, and package pickup.

Dining
Sunnyside Café – Quick Service location. Offers a buffet breakfast for ¥158 per adult and ¥108 per child. Lunch is a la carte and offers noodles, dim sum, stew, grill options such as chicken legs, pork chops and roasted eel. Dinner is a buffet at ¥198 per adult + ¥25 for unlimited drinks or + ¥40 for unlimited beer; the child price is ¥138. Closes at 8:30pm, so not an option after returning from the theme park.
Sunnyside Market – Snack location/cafe. Café-style location serving hot drinks, juices, yogurts and ice cream, snacks such as popcorn and potato chips, sandwiches, fruit and alcoholic drinks.

Tickets

There are many ways to buy park entry tickets for the Shanghai Disney Resort. Prices, special offers and ticket lengths vary depending on where you buy your tickets. To help you choose the best option for you, here is a detailed look at your ticket options.

Online Tickets and Tickets at the Park

Important: If you have booked a combined hotel and ticket package through the Shanghai Disney Resort website, you can skip this section, as your tickets are included in your package unless you specifically make a room-only reservation.

Guests should purchase tickets in advance online. The theme park does sell out of tickets on peak days, so it is worth buying these as soon as possible. Compared to the Western Disney theme parks, tickets here are relatively cheap.

The easiest place to buy the tickets (up to 1 month in advance) is the official website at shanghaidisneyresort.com/en. You must have a passport with the same name as that on the tickets to gain access to the park on the day of your visit.

You can also buy tickets on other reseller websites such as Klook at bit.ly/sdrtics (this ticket also includes a meal in the park). You can get an exclusive discount on your first booking by signing up at this special link - bit.ly/klookref.

Finally, if you are staying at a Disney hotel, then you can buy the tickets at the hotel itself when you arrive, paying with either cash or card. You will be guaranteed entry to the parks with a hotel stay and get an extra Fastpass.

You can purchase a theme park ticket for one or two days.

Pricing is based on the date that you visit and you can check up to 90 days in advance which pricing tier your ticket will fall into onto the Shanghai Disney Resort website.

A 2-day ticket must be used on two consecutive days and offers a 10-20% discount over buying two single-day tickets.

A discount of around 25% is available for children (aged 3 to 11 years old or with a

height between 1.01m and up 1.4 meters), seniors (65 years old and above) and guests with disabilities (certificate/proof of disability is required).

Infants (under the age of 3 years old or with a height of 1.0 meter and below) will continue to receive free admission.

Standard Ticket Prices – Until 5th June 2020
Regular: ¥399
Peak: ¥575
Holiday Peak: ¥665

Standard Ticket Prices – From 6th June 2020
Regular: ¥399
Regular Plus: ¥499
Peak: ¥599
Peak Plus: ¥699

Annual Passes

Another option you may wish to consider is getting an Annual Pass to the park as it works out to be a good deal for extended visits. It is also a good way to save money if you visit two or more times within a year (e.g. visiting in August 2020 and then July 2021).

There are three main types of pass – Silver, Gold and Diamond.

Silver Pass

1,299 CNY for adults and 974 CNY for ages 3 to 11, seniors (65 and older) and disabled guests

Silver Pass benefits:
● Access to the park for at least 45 days of the year (mostly Sundays).
● 20% off dining at the theme park and resort hotels
● Free birthday cake
● Occasional discounts on Shanghai Disney Resort hotel room rates
● Shopping and dining benefits in Disneytown

Gold Pass

1,599 CNY for adults and 1,199 CNY for ages 3 to 11, seniors (65 and older) and disabled guests

Gold Pass benefits:
● Access to the park for at least 250 days of the year (including most weekdays, Sundays, and part of the Summer and Winter holidays).
● All the Silver Pass benefits
● Buy two get one free buffet dinner at Shanghai Disney Resort's Lumière's Kitchen
● Buy dinner at Aurora and get a free bottle of wine

Diamond Pass

3,299 CNY for adults and 2,474 CNY for ages 3 to 11, seniors (65 and older) and disabled guests

Diamond Pass benefits:
● Access to the park every day of the year
● All the Silver and Gold Pass benefits
● 20% off parking
● Early Park Entry up to 12 times per year
● Free stroller rental up to 4 times per year
● Priority access to exclusive events

You can view the annual pass date calendar up to 3 months in advance at www.shanghaidisneyresort.com/en/annual-pass/. If the dates work for you, the Gold Pass can usually pay for itself in two to three days – you could consider only buying one annual pass to avail of the discounts and buying regular tickets for the rest of your party.

Top Tip: The annual pass start date is 15 days after the date of purchase if bought online or on the app. Make sure to only buy it a few days in advance of your visit, or on the day at the theme park itself.

Top Tip 2: You can use your price of a 1-day admission ticket towards an annual pass if you upgrade on the day of your visit at Guest Relations (you only pay the difference). Sometimes there is even a promotion where you get one free Disney Premier Access when doing this.

Early Park Entry Pass Ticket

Shanghai Disney Resort offers a 1-hour early entry add-on for ¥159 – during this time selected park attractions are open. There is a dedicated park entrance area by the main turnstiles for this Early Access add-on – this can be purchased via WeChat and the Shanghai Disney Resort app up to 4 days in advance. This is a great way to get into the park before the general crowds, and even before the on-site hotels. If you are staying on-site at a Disney hotel, and are already getting 30 minutes early entry, we would not say this is necessary.

If you are visiting during a busy time or are staying off-site then this is good value for money as you will be able to experience several major attractions within the first hour before the park opens to the public.

Chapter Seven | Understanding the Parks

Understanding the Parks

Before taking a detailed look at the theme park, we think it is best to explain some of the services on offer at Shanghai Disneyland, including Fastpass, Single Rider queue lines, the Shanghai Disney Resort app, and more.

When to Visit

Crowds at Shanghai Disney Resort vary significantly from season to season and even day to day. The difference in a single day can save you thousands of yuan and hours in queue lines. You need to consider national and school holidays in China and surrounding countries, the weather, pricing, and more to find the best time to go.

Here is our guide of the best times to visit Shanghai Disney Resort, even including a detailed analysis of weekdays.

Major Holidays In 2020 (Times to Avoid)
• 1st to 5th January: New Year's Day & School Break
• 24th to 30th January: Chinese New Year
• 28th March to 5th April: School Holidays
• 1st to 3rd May: Labor Day Weekend
• 25th to 28th June: Dragon Boat Festival Weekend
• Mid-June to start of September: Summer School Holidays
• 25th September to 7th October: Mid-Autumn Festival and Golden Week
• 12th December 2020 to 4th January 2021 – Winter School Holidays

Ideal times to visit are therefore: most of January to March, April, May, early June, early and mid-September, mid-October to mid-December. Watch out for any holidays above, though.

Days of the Week
The days of the week that you visit make a tremendous difference to how long you will wait to get on rides. A ride can have a wait time of 90 minutes on one day, and just 30 minutes the next. The most notable difference is between weekends and weekdays.

The best days of the week to visit are Tuesday, Wednesday and Thursday, then Friday, then Monday. Saturday and Sunday are busy year-round – with Sunday being slightly less busy usually. Park hours are often longer on weekends to compensate for the larger crowds. Weekends should be avoided throughout the year unless it is your only way to visit.

Specific Dates
As well as the above information to guide your visit, you can use the Shanghai Disneyland website to simulate purchasing tickets – this allows you to see the pricing calendar. The higher the price, the higher the expected attendance for that date.

18 The Independent Guide to Shanghai Disneyland 2020

Shanghai Disney Resort App

The Shanghai Disney Resort has a free Apple iOS and Android app, which allows you to enhance your trip.

You can check the opening hours, timings of shows and parades, book Fastpass, buy an Early Park Entry Pass, buy Disney Premier Access, buy park tickets, and even see the attraction wait times.

You will need a data connection to see live information, which means you must connect to the in-park Wi-Fi or use a data connection.

The app is translated into English for your convenience.

On-Ride Photos

Some of Shanghai Disney Resort's rides have cameras positioned and timed to take perfect on-ride photos of you at the most action-filled moments on attractions. Buy the picture and see yourself at the fastest, steepest, scariest, and most fun moment of the ride. These make for timeless keepsakes.

When you get off selected rides, you will walk past screens that preview your photo (with a watermark on top). If you wish to purchase it, go to the photo counter.

You do not have to buy on-ride photos straight after your ride; you can pick them up at any time that same day. Just remember your unique number at the ride exit or ask a member of staff at the photo kiosk to write it down for you.

If you like the photo, Cast Members will show it to you up close before you pay for it. If you like it, buy it! You will treasure the photo for a long time.

You can get on-ride photos included with other park photos as part of Photopass - see page 23.

The attractions with on-ride photos are *Pirates of the Caribbean, TRON,* and *Buzz Lightyear Planet Rescue*.

Package Pickup

The Package Pickup Service allows you to buy an item at any of the theme park shops and pick it up later.

When paying for your goods, ask to use the Package Pickup Service. You will leave the item with the Cast Member who served you. When you have finished your day at the park, you can pick up your item.

You can then either pick up your purchases at Guest Services after the turnstiles (to the left after the turnstiles) outside the park from 1:00pm, or at the Disney shops at the Disney hotels.

This means that you can collect all your items in one spot, even if you have multiple items from different shops.

If you are sending items back to the hotel, this service stops at 4:00pm – if sending the items to Guest Services at the park, then this service stops at 6:00pm.

This service allows you to be free to eat, shop, ride attractions and watch shows to your heart's content without carrying any bags.

Understanding the Parks

Fastpass

The Shanghai Disney Resort offers a unique skip-the-queue system called Fastpass at no cost. It allows you to reserve a time slot for certain attractions, return at an appointed time, and ride with little to no wait. While waiting for your Fastpass reservation time, you can do something else such as shop, dine, watch a show, or experience another attraction.

How to use Fastpass

1. Find a Fastpass ride
You can identify rides that offer Fastpass (FP) by the FP logo on park maps. It is helpful to know which attractions offer Fastpass in advance by reading through this guide and looking at the park map.

2. Check the wait time using the app and decide
In the app use the map to see an overview of all the rides, and how long the wait for each one is.

At the entrance to each ride, there is a screen showing what time Fastpasses are being issued for - e.g. 10:25 to 11:25.

If the wait is too long for you, then you should use the FP system. If the standby wait is less than 30 minutes, we recommend waiting in the standby queue. This is because Fastpasses often require you to backtrack across the park negating time savings.

3. Get your Fastpass
Open the Shanghai Disney Resort app. Tap the Mickey Head and under 'Make Plans' tap 'Get Fastpass'. Choose the tickets of the people who you would like to book a Fastpass for on the next screen. Then choose which ride you would like to get a Fastpass for – the time of the Fastpass will be shown. Tap 'confirm'.

You will see a confirmation screen and be told what time you can make your next Fastpass from.

4. Wait
Dine, explore the park, or enjoy another ride or show until your FP return time.

5. Return and Ride
Return to the ride during the time window on your FP, entering through the ride's Fastpass entrance. At the FastPass ride entrance, scan your digital Fastpass at the reader.

Later in the queue, you may need to scan your Fastpass a second time on another reader. Now, you can ride within a few minutes, skipping the regular queue – the wait time with a Fastpass is usually under 10 minutes, but can be up to 15 minutes.

Note: We highly recommend using the Shanghai Disney Resort app to book Fastpasses. If you do not or cannot use the app, then you have the backup of a paper system. When the park opened, the idea was that you would visit 'Guest Services' stations in each land with kiosks and select a Fastpass reservation for any ride in that land. Since the introduction of digital Fastpass, this has been widely phased out and most of the kiosks are closed. Disney on its official website even says to visit the

Adventure Isle Guest Service location to book your paper Fastpass. We highly recommend using the digital system as the park is huge and you do not want to have to walk all the way across the park each time you want to make a Fastpass reservation.

Preparing for Fastpass with the Shanghai Disney Resort App

Save yourself the hassle of paper Fastpass tickets by using the free Shanghai Disney Resort app.

Make sure to download this app and create an account before arriving at Shanghai Disneyland to make the most of your time there.

As soon as you are in the park, click the Mickey head icon, then 'My Tickets and Annual Passes' and then 'Link Tickets & Passes.' Then scan your park ticket QR code. Do this for your whole party on one smartphone.

Note: If you bought your park tickets on the app, your tickets may be linked automatically.

The Fastpass System Explained

Now that you have read about the advantages of the Fastpass system, we have to tell you the system's limitations - namely that you cannot use Fastpasses to avoid every single wait.

Firstly, not every ride offers Fastpass - only 7 out of 30+ attractions at the park offer this service.

Secondly, you can only hold one Fastpass ticket (and therefore only skip one queue) at a time, though there are exceptions to this as noted on the next page. You will only use Fastpass throughout your time at the Shanghai Disney Resort a limited number of times.

How Fastpass works:
Every Shanghai Disney Resort theme park entry ticket and annual pass includes Fastpass – it is a free system for every guest.

Each day, the park will decide what percentage of riders will be able to use the Fastpass system. Let's say that in this case, it is 50%.

So, assuming 2000 guests per hour can ride *TRON Lightcycle Power Run*, the Fastpass system will distribute 1000 Fastpass tickets for each operating hour. This means 50% of guests will use Fastpass to board the ride, and 50% will use the regular standby queue each hour.

There are, therefore, a limited number of Fastpass tickets for each ride each hour. This is to ensure that the standby queue line is kept to a reasonable level.

The first Fastpass return time for an attraction is usually 30 minutes after park opening, although sometimes it is later.

Fastpass slots then move in 5-minute increments, so after all the Fastpasses for 10:30am-11:30am are distributed, the next return time will be 10:35am-11:35am.

Once all Fastpasses have been distributed for the day, your luck is up. You will have to use the standby queue line or Single Rider queue line (if available). For some rides you can also essentially pay for a Fastpass with a system called *Disney Premier Access* which is discussed on the next page.

Rides may not offer Fastpasses for the entire park operating hours for a variety of reasons.

If you want to know the time of the last Fastpass return, ask the Cast Members at the attraction. When Fastpass stops being used, the regular queue moves much more quickly.

Due to the limited number of Fastpasses available, tickets often run out on popular rides early in the day. This happens regularly on Soaring Over the Horizon and Roaring Rapids. These often disappear within the first hour of the park opening.

On busy days, all rides will distribute the daily allocation of Fastpasses within 2-3 hours of opening.

Is Fastpass available daily?
Yes.

Good to Know
Soaring Over the Horizon has a pre-show. Then, you enter a short queue line to board the ride, but the wait may be up to 20 minutes. On other rides, you should be on the ride in under 10 minutes.

Get Extra Fastpasses

Officially, you can only hold one Fastpass at a time. However, there are exceptions.

• When your Fastpass return time begins, you can get another Fastpass even if you have not used your current Fastpass yet. E.g., You have a Roaring Rapids Fastpass for 14:00-15:00. You can get another Fastpass from 14:00.

• If your return time is over two hours away, you can get a second Fastpass two hours after picking up the first. E.g., You got a *Soaring Over the Horizon* Fastpass reservation at 9:00; the return time is 15:00-16:00. As 15:00 is over two hours away from when you got your Fastpass reservation, you can get another Fastpass reservation at 11:00 (two hours after 9:00). You can check the time your next Fastpass is available on the app or at the bottom of your latest Fastpass reminder ticket.

Fastpass Attractions List

• TRON Lightcycle Power Run
• Buzz Lightyear Planet Rescue
• Seven Dwarfs Mine Train
• Peter Pan's Flight
• The Many Adventures of Winnie the Pooh
• Soaring Over the Horizon
• Roaring Rapids

Fastpass Availability

Not every Fastpass is created equal – there are some attractions which are more popular than others, some attractions distribute more Fastpasses than others, and some Fastpasses will save you more time than others.

In order of the most valuable to least valuable Fastpasses:
• Soaring Over the Horizon
• Roaring Rapids
• TRON Lightcycle Power Run
• Seven Dwarfs Mine Train
• Buzz Lightyear Planet Rescue
• Peter Pan's Flight
• The Many Adventures of Winnie the Pooh

Disney Premier Access

Disney Premier Access is essentially a paid-for Fastpass, giving you priority access to select attractions in the theme park.

Disney Premier Access is available for all the Fastpass attractions listed above. Plus, it is also available for:
• Rex's Racer
• Woody's Roundup
• Voyage to the Crystal Grotto
• Pirates of the Caribbean
• Challenge Trails at Camp Discovery

For the Fastpass-enabled attractions, you will gain access through the Fastpass entrance. For the five others, there is a dedicated Premier Access entrance. Unlike Fastpass, there is no specific time slot you have to use your Premier Access – you can use each Premier Access whenever you want.

You can buy Premier Access in the app or at select shops in each land. Prices vary according to demand but are around ¥120 to ¥150 for one ride, or ¥650 for a set of several. Premier Access for individual rides does sell out, and can only be purchased when in the park.

Top Tip: If you buy a set for multiple attractions, you get Premier Access for all rides, even if these are sold out for individual purchases.

Of all the above attractions, we would only really consider Disney Premier Access valuable for *Soaring Over the Horizon*, *Roaring Rapids*, *Challenge Trails at Camp Discovery* and *Seven Dwarfs Mine Train* in that order, with *Soaring* being the most necessary, and only if there is no Fastpass available, of course – *Seven Dwarfs* also has the option of Single Rider.

Photopass

Shanghai Disneyland's Photopass is an easy to use system that makes collecting all your in-park photos easy.

Simply go to any in-park photographer (including those with characters) and after your photo is taken, they will scan your park ticket associating that photo with your account. You can also do this at any ride photo counter. Alternatively, you can ask for a Photopass card instead of scanning your park ticket.

Next time you have a photo taken, hand over your park ticket or Photopass card and the pictures will be added onto it throughout your visit and be kept together on the system. You can keep doing this anywhere you find a photographer or with on-ride photos.

You can also add extra Disney magic with themed borders and details at no additional cost.

Photos are saved on the Photopass system for 30 days each from when they were taken.

Before your photos expire, visit one of the locations noted on your park map to view and purchase your photos. At all these locations, you can purchase prints or digital versions of your Photopass photos.

Alternatively, if you only want digital photos, download the Shanghai Disney Photopass app (separate from the resort app).

Pricing is ¥59 per digital photo, or ¥199 for all digital photos from one park ticket for 1 day. If you want printed photos these are ¥99 to ¥129 each for the first photo, and ¥80 for

subsequent photos. Each printed photo also includes the same photo in a digital format at no extra cost.

For those who have used Photopass or Memory Maker in the American parks or at Disneyland Paris, the Shanghai Disneyland system is similar.

The most significant difference, however, is the lower number of Photopass photographers throughout the parks in China whereas there are many of them in each park in the US, allowing you to get great photos with the parks' icons.

Rider Switch

A common issue at theme parks is when two adults want to ride an attraction, but they have a child who is not tall enough to ride. There are three solutions:
a) the adults can take turns to ride (queuing twice);
b) one adult can choose not to experience the attraction;
c) skip the attraction.

The solution is Disney's Rider Switch, which allows one adult to queue up and ride while the other stays with the child.

Each attraction implements the system in a slightly different manner so ask Cast Members at ride entrances for details.

Generally speaking, the party asks the Cast Member at the ride entrance to use Rider Switch. Enter the line with your entire party, except those not riding the first time. One or two adults will wait with the non-rider in the Rider Switch area. The remainder of the party will experience the attraction. When the remainder of the party returns to the Rider Switch area, the guest(s) who waited with the non-rider take their turn using the Fastpass entrance or alternative entrance.

If this is the case of two adults with a child, each adult will experience the ride separately, but the second adult will not need to wait to ride.

You do not need to have a child or baby to use this service. You could use it to stay with an adult who does not wish to ride.

Understanding the Parks

Single Rider

One of the best ways to significantly reduce your time waiting for attractions is to use the Single Rider queue instead of the regular standby queue. This is available at selected attractions at the resort.

The Single Rider queue fills free spaces on ride vehicles. For example, if a ride vehicle can seat 8 people and a group of 4 turns up, followed by a group of 3, then a Single Rider will fill the free space.

This allows guests who are willing to ride with strangers to experience a shorter wait, and fills a space. This system reduces waits for all.

Single Rider queues may be closed when waits in that queue are too long, or when the theme park is not busy.

Single Rider Lines can be used by groups too, but members of the group will be separated, and each will ride in a different vehicle. You can, of course, wait for each other after riding by the exit but you will not ride together.

The following attractions operate Single Rider Lines:
• TRON Lightcycle Power Run
• Seven Dwarfs Mine Train
• Pirates of the Caribbean

To use Single Rider simply ask the Cast Member at the ride entrance, they will direct you to a separate queue line and give you a Single Rider ticket, which you will need to hand to a Cast Member later in the queue - you may also be directed to the Fastpass queue instead and be given this same Single Rider ticket.

Early Park Entry

Early Park Entry allows guests staying at the two Disney hotels (Shanghai Disneyland Hotel and Toy Story Hotel) early theme park access to selected attractions at Shanghai Disneyland for 30 minutes each morning.

Guests get access to an almost empty park, ride with little to no wait, and, importantly, can make FastPass reservations for popular rides before the general public enters the park. 30 minutes may not sound like much, but this little benefit can really improve your enjoyment of the theme park in setting you up for a fantastic day and skipping one or two long waits for rides.

Using Early Park Entry
Disney hotel guests will need their park ticket, passport and their room key. Hotel shuttle buses will drop off guests at Disneytown in the morning as this is where the 'secret' priority entrance into the park is located. If you are walking from the hotel, you will need to go here. This is a much more pleasant experience than the chaos to go through security at the main theme park entrance. This entrance lets you in right by Tomorrowland, skipping the park's entrance area, Mickey Avenue.

What is open during Early Park Entry?
The content of Early Park Entry changes according to operational needs on the day, but includes most of the park's major attractions.

The typical line-up includes: *Soaring Over the Horizon, TRON Lightcycle Power Run, Buzz Lightyear Planet Rescue, Peter Pan's Flight, Seven Dwarfs Mine Train, The Many Adventures of Winnie the Pooh, Pirates of the Caribbean - Battle for the Sunken Treasure, Rex's Racer,* and *Woody's Roundup.*

Can I get in even earlier?
Yes, there is a paid option available to all guests (including non-hotel guests) called the Early Park Entry Pass. This allows you to get in 1 hour before regular park admission – this is 30 minutes before even hotel guests get entry. The only caveat is you must use the main entrance to the theme park and not the Disneytown entrance.

The cost of Early Park Entry is ¥159, which we think is excellent value (especially if it is busy), and it can be purchased in the app. Disney recommends getting to the park 90 minutes before the regular park opening time so you can clear security and make the most of your 1-hour early entry.

What should I do during Early Park Entry?
If your aim is to maximize your time and you ride all types of rides, then:

• With 30 minutes early entry: Get a Fastpass for *Soaring*, ride *TRON*, then ride *Seven Dwarfs Mine Train*, then wait outside the entrance to *Roaring Rapids* or *Challenge Trails* just before the park opens to everyone.
• With 1-hour early entry: Get a Fastpass for *Soaring*, ride *TRON*, ride *Seven Dwarfs Mine Train*, ride *Pirates of the Caribbean - Battle for the Sunken Treasure*, then wait outside the entrance to *Roaring Rapids* or *Challenge Trails* just before the park opens to everyone.

Disney Concierge Services

If you want to upgrade your park experience, Shanghai Disney Resort offers a series of benefits in one package. This may be worth considering on very busy days.

Benefits include:
• Entry via the Disneytown entrance
• Early entry into the theme park
• Disney Premier Access to *Soaring Over the Horizon, Roaring Rapids, TRON Lightcycle Power Run, Buzz Lightyear Planet Rescue, Peter Pan's Flight, Seven Dwarfs Mine Train, The Many Adventures of Winnie the Pooh* and *Pirates of the Caribbean: Battle for the Sunken Treasure* in the classic package.
• The deluxe package also includes Disney Premier Access to *Rex's Racer, Woody's Roundup, Challenge Trails at Camp Discovery, Voyage to the Crystal Grotto* in addition to the above.
• Reserved Viewing Areas:

Watch *Mickey's Storybook Express parade* and the *Ignite the Dream Nighttime Spectacular* from reserved viewing areas.
• Convenient Dining: Enjoy priority seating at Quick Service restaurants, and express pick up for turkey drums at select distribution points (subject to availability).
• Premium Planning: Make the most of your trip with exclusive concierge services standing by to help with any of your inquiries.

Prices vary according to the date of visit and can be booked at shanghaidisneyresort.com/en/.

This is an excellent package, but even on busy days you can accomplish visiting most of the park using our Touring Plan (see later in this guide) and simply purchasing Early Park Entry. This does give you more flexibility though with all the reserved viewing areas and access to rides, so it is worth considering for the ease of use!

Disney Premier Tours

If you want the ultimate VIP treatment, be prepared to pay for it. Shanghai Disney Resort is happy to oblige with its Premier Tour service, often used by celebrities, those who don't wish to wait for anything, or for guests who are very short on time.

The tour lasts for six consecutive hours and is offered for groups of 3 to 8 guests. Included in the price:

• Your private VIP tour guide for just your party who will share facts and details about the park
• Dedicated VIP entrance into Shanghai Disneyland
• Expedited access into all attractions and shows
• Reserved entertainment spots for daytime performances, *Mickey's Storybook Express* parade and the *Ignite the Dream* nighttime spectacular
• Discount on merchandise

Pricing varies by date but is generally around ¥16,000 to ¥24,000 per party. This does not include the theme park entry tickets which are extra.

To learn more about Premier Tour Services, or to make a reservation, contact the VIP Reservation Center by phone on +86 (21)-2060-3366.

Wheelchair and Stroller Rentals

Wheelchair and stroller rentals are available for guests who do not wish to bring their own.

If your child is recently out of a stroller, it is often still worth renting one as it is likely they will get tired, due to the vast walking distances involved with a Shanghai Disney Resort visit.

Sometimes it is nice just to let kids sit in their stroller and have a break. The stroller can also be used as an easy way to carry bags.

The daily cost of hiring a stroller or a wheelchair is ¥90. The rental location is to the left after the turnstiles, before entering Mickey Avenue.

You are, of course, welcome to bring your own stroller or wheelchair if you wish.

When experiencing attractions, be sure to leave your stroller in the dedicated parking areas. Ask a Cast Member if you are not sure whether this is. Strollers may be moved by Cast Members to keep them neat and organized.

Lockers

There are coin-operated lockers available both inside and outside the theme park.

At Shanghai Disneyland, these are at Mickey Avenue, *Tron*, *Roaring Rapids* and *Camp Discovery*.

Locker fees are:
• Medium Locker at Mickey Avenue, *Tron* and *Roaring Rapids* – ¥60 per day
• Large Locker at Mickey Avenue, *Tron* and *Roaring Rapids* – ¥80 per day
• Medium Locker at *Camp Discovery* – Free for 2 hours, then ¥50 per hour, up to ¥300 per day.
• Large Locker at *Camp Discovery* – Free for 2 hours, then ¥70 per hour, up to ¥420 per day.

The *Camp Discovery* lockers are designed to only be used while queuing and experiencing that attraction, hence why they are free for 2 hours and then there is a hefty fee.

Payment is accepted by cash, Union Pay cards, Alipay and WeChat Pay.

If you have luggage, this cannot enter the park. Luggage Storage facilities are available in the parking lot near Group Services, and to the right of the turnstiles at the main entrance of Shanghai Disneyland for luggage and larger items that are not permitted in the theme park.

Small items with total dimensions (i.e. length plus width plus height) not exceeding 60cm cost just ¥10 to store. Oversized items, such as luggage, are ¥80 per item.

Spend Less Time Waiting in Queue Lines

The Shanghai Disney Resort meticulously themes its queues to introduce an attraction's story before you board. However, no one likes waiting, and often you want to ride as quickly as possible. Remember that a visit to a theme park will involve waiting in queue lines; this chapter covers our top tips on minimizing these waits.

1. Eat outside the regular dining hours
At Shanghai Disney Resort, whether you want to eat at a Table Service restaurant or a Quick Service meal, waiting for your food is part of the game. Have lunch before midday or after 3:00 pm for much shorter waits. Also, having dinner before 7:00 pm will reduce your time waiting. Waits of 20 minutes or longer to order are relatively typical at peak times at Quick Service restaurants.

2. Quick Service meal tricks
At Quick Service locations, each cashier has two queues, and alternates between them – count how many groups (families or friends) are in front of you in the queue. There may be ten people in front of you in one queue line but only two families. The other queue line may have five people but from five different families. The queue with ten people will move more quickly with only two orders to process versus the other queue's five orders.

3. On-site Disney hotel guests
If you are staying at a Disney hotel at the Shanghai Disney Resort, take advantage of Early Park Entry. You get admission into the theme park 30 minutes before regular guests do. Although this may not sound like much, using this time wisely will allow you to ride one or two popular attractions and get a Fastpass, saving you several hours straight away. See our Early Park Entry section for more details.

4. Get to the parks before opening time
If the park opens at 8:00 am, you should be at the park entrance at least 60 minutes before so that you can be as close to the front of the queue as possible and clear security – the main entrance is extremely busy. The same applies to Early Park Entry, get there about 15 minutes early to be as close to the front as possible.

5. Use FastPass and Single Rider
Earlier in this section, we covered the Fastpass system in detail. This is a free system, and you must use it to minimize waits effectively. You should be able to get at least 3 Fastpasses each day through proper planning. See our chapter entitled 'Touring Plans' for more details on how to maximize your time at the park. Plus, you can also use Single Rider queue lines to save a lot of time (see page 24).

6. Skip the parades and fireworks
If you have already seen the parades, shows, or fireworks, use that time to experience rides as the wait times are often shorter during these big events – this mainly applies to the nighttime spectaculars and the daytime parade. If you have not seen the park's entertainment offerings before, we recommend you watch these. Parades and shows are only performed at set times of the day, and most of these are as good as, if not better than, many rides.

Understanding the Parks

If there are two parade performances on the day of your visit, generally the second performance has fewer guests watching.

7. Ride outdoor attractions when it rains
Outdoor attractions such as *Dumbo, Roaring Rapids,* and *Seven Dwarfs Mine Train* (mostly outdoors) often have significantly reduced waits when it is raining. Yes, you may get wet while riding (a jacket will help), but the wait times will be shorter. In contrast, avoid the indoor rides when there is inclement weather as the waits will be artificially longer.

8. Choose when to visit carefully
Visit during an off-peak time if possible. If you are visiting on New Year's Day, expect to queue a lot longer than in the middle of February. Of course, weekends are busier than weekdays. See our 'When to Visit' section to make the most of your time.

9. Shop at the end of the day
Go shopping at the end of the day. Even when the park is 'officially' closed, the shops by the park entrance areas stay open longer than the rest of the park. Alternatively, go to Disneytown in the evening or your hotel's Disney shop, which are all open late. Shop at strategic times, and make the most of your time in the parks.

10. Get a Times Guide
Get your Park Map and the 'Today' Times Guide on the way in; you will usually find them distributed together. The 'Today' Times Guide lists all time-sensitive information at the parks such as the timings of parades, shows, character appearances, and more. As such, you will not waste time crossing the park to find out that a character you saw earlier in the day has now left a particular location.

11. Throw money at the problem
All the above solutions are free, but there are various time-saving packages that will cost you money. Perhaps the best value is the Early Park Entry Pass which gets you into the park one hour before regular guests. You can also purchase priority admission with Disney Premier Access and get a package with all this and more with a Concierge Service package.

Doing Disney on a Budget

A visit to Shanghai Disney Resort can be pricey. However, there are ways to reduce your spending at the resort and still have a magical time.

1. Hotels – Disney hotels are themed, have Early Park Entry and other benefits but are also much more expensive than other hotels, such as those a few metro stations away, or a short taxi ride away (see our hotels section for other hotel recommendations). These outside hotels are a fraction of the price.

2. Eat at Disneytown – Disneytown is a giant entertainment and dining area located on Disney property near the resort's entrance. The food here is often cheaper than the food in the theme parks. See our Disneytown section for more details.

3. Take your own photos – If you do not want to pay for an 'official' Disney character photo, take one yourself; the Cast Members do not mind. They will even take the photo for you!

4. Take your own gifts – Buy dresses, outfits, and toys outside of Shanghai Disney from Disney Stores, online, or at supermarkets before you visit the resort. Give your child the costume on

arrival to avoid the high in-park merchandise prices.

5. More affordable meals – Although food prices are high, some restaurants offer better value than others – generally those selling Chinese food instead of Western food offer the best value. Try the set menus or a buffet as a late lunch and having a lighter dinner. Also, don't buy a whole set menu – most items can be purchased individually.

6. Park Tickets – We recommend you purchase your tickets in advance. You can either do this at the official Shanghai Disney Resort website or from other retailers. The park uses seasonal pricing so you can get a ticket for ¥399 on a less crowded day instead of ¥699 on a busier day.

7. Take Snacks – According to park rules, you can absolutely bring your own food and drink into the park, unlike at Tokyo Disney Resort, for example. The exact wording Disney uses is: "Guests are allowed to bring outside food and beverage items into the Park for self-consumption, provided that they do not require heating, reheating, processing, refrigeration or temperature control and do not have pungent odors. Examples of food items not permitted in the Park include, without limitation, instant noodles that require hot water, food kept in containers with reheating capabilities, and durian fruit."

There are also water fountains in the park to refill with water throughout the day – Disney says the tap water at its theme park is safe to drink, which is not the case in Shanghai itself.

Meeting the Characters

For many visitors, meeting characters is the highlight of their trip. Playing with Pluto, talking to Cinderella, and hugging Mickey makes for magical memories.

Unlike the other Disney parks, there are not really any free-roaming characters and you will find characters at dedicated meet and greet areas with organized queuing systems.

Shanghai Disneyland
Certain characters are scheduled to appear around the park throughout the day. Times will appear on the official park app.

At *Happy Circle* in Adventure Isle, you can find King Louie, Baloo, Rafiki and Timon. Sometimes you can also find characters from Zootopia here.

At *Meeting Post* in Toy Story Land, you can find Woody and Jessie.

At *Storybook Court* in Fantasyland, you can find the Disney princesses including Cinderella, Rapunzel, Belle and Snow White.

In the Gardens of Imagination, you can meet Mickey Mouse and Marvel Superheroes including Captain America and Spider-Man.

In Mickey Avenue, you can meet Minnie Mouse and some of her friends, which could include Mickey, Donald, Daisy, Goofy, Pluto and Chip 'n Dale.

In Tomorrowland, you can meet The Avengers at *Avengers Training Initiative*, and Baymax at the *E-Stage*.

Finally, in Treasure Cove you can meet Jack Sparrow at *Sparrow Nest*.

Hotels
Characters are present at both the Disney hotels. At *Toy Story Hotel*, there are no character dining opportunities but you can often see Woody and Jessie in the lobby.

At *Shanghai Disneyland Hotel*, you can also often find various Disney characters in the lobby, as well as at the character buffet at Lumiere's Kitchen.

Ride Height Requirements

Certain attractions at both theme parks have minimum height requirements to ride for safety reasons. These are strict and will not be bent for anyone – no matter if your child is just 0.5cm too short, these height restrictions are here for safety and are set in stone.

Here we list all of the current ride height requirements for your easy reference.

- Explorer Canoes – Feet must touch the floor when seated
- Woody's Roundup – 81cm
- Seven Dwarfs Mine Train – 97cm
- Soaring Over the Horizon – 102cm
- Challenge Trails at Camp Discovery – 106cm
- Roaring Rapids – 107cm
- Jet Packs – 112cm
- Fantasia Carousel – 120cm to ride alone (none to ride accompanied)
- Rex's Racer – 120cm
- TRON Lightcycle Power Run – 122cm

Do remember that just because your child may meet the height requirement doesn't necessarily mean that they won't be scared of the ride, and vice-versa.

Park Rules and Etiquette

Shanghai Disney Resort has several rules and regulations regarding how to watch park entertainment, such as parades, shows, and nighttime spectaculars. These are in place to ensure everyone has the best experience.

Key points include:
- For everyone's safety when taking photos or videos, please refrain from using equipment such as monopods, tripods, or selfie sticks (hand-size grip attachments are permitted).

- The following items, among others, cannot be brought into the park: flammable items; weapons; food items which require heating, reheating, processing, refrigeration or temperature control, food items which have pungent odors (Examples of food items not permitted in the Park include, without limitation, instant noodles that require hot water, food kept in containers with reheating capabilities, and durian fruit); alcoholic beverages; cans or glass containers; oversized luggage; large tripods; folding chairs and stools; animals; articles prohibited by applicable laws and other items that may be harmful or disruptive.

- Costumes may not be worn by guests age 16 or older. Clothing that drags on the ground is prohibited.

- Masks may not be worn by guests age 16 or older (unless they are for medical purposes). Masks must be worn in a way that both eyes can be fully seen and with unobstructed vision at all times allowing for clear peripheral lines of sight.

- With the exception of designated smoking areas, smoking of tobacco, e-cigarettes or other products that produce a vapor or smoke is not allowed in the Park.

- Guests under age 16 must be accompanied by a guest age 16 or older to enter the Park.

- To board an attraction, children under age 7 must be accompanied by a person age 16 or older.

- Animals (except guide dogs) are not permitted inside the park. Guide dogs must remain on a leash or in a harness and under the control of the owner at all times. Due to the nature of some attractions, guide dogs may not be permitted to ride certain attractions.

The rules are strict as we have found that guest behavior at Shanghai Disneyland is the poorest out of all the Disney parks in the world. That is not to say it is bad, but we do wish they would take an even stricter and more orderly approach like that taken at the Tokyo Disney Resort.

Chapter Eight | Dining

Dining

There are a variety of places to eat at the Shanghai Disney Resort. Food options vary from sandwich and snack locations to Quick Service (fast food) places, character buffets, Table Service dining and even fine dining options. Eating can be as much a part of the experience as the attractions at the Shanghai Disney Resort.

Making Reservations

To guarantee you can dine at a specific Table Service restaurant, it is worth booking a table in advance. There is only one Table Service restaurant in the park – *Royal Banquet Hall* (a Table Service character dining experience). At Shanghai Disneyland Hotel, there are two restaurants you can book: *Lumieres Kitchen* (a character dining buffet) and *Aurora* (a Table Service restaurant).

With a Disney hotel reservation, you can make your restaurant either in advance or at the resort. The restaurants also take walk-ins and same-day reservations subject to availability.

There is no option to pre-purchase meal credits. Each restaurant is paid for on the day at the restaurant when dining.

Some Table Service restaurants in Disneytown accept reservations directly.

Top Tip: To dine at *Royal Banquet Hall*, specifically, it is worth booking in advance - it is popular.

Restaurant Types

Buffet – All-you-can-eat locations where you fill your plate from the selection as many times as you want.

Quick Service – Fast food. Look at the menus, pay and collect your food. You will find everything from burgers and fries, to chicken, to pizza and pasta. Be aware that Disney 'fast'-food locations are notoriously slow. Most restaurants at the resort are Quick Service restaurants.

Table Service – Order from a waiter who brings your food to your table.

Character Buffets – All-you-can-eat places where characters interact with you and take photos as you eat.

Top Tip: You usually do not have to order from a set menu. Ordering specific items 'a la carte' is completely fine, although it may save you money if you order certain set menu combinations.

Top Tip 2: The 'set meals' at Shanghai Disneyland Quick Service locations are referred to as "combos", so if you only want a burger which is in a set meal ask the Cast Member for "burger only – no combo" to help them understand.

Snacks

A huge part of Disney and theme park culture is snacking You may well find that you can skip a meal and have several snacks instead.

Here are some of the most popular:
• **Donald Waffles** – Just like a Mickey waffle, but Donald themed. Sold at *Il Paperino*, Mickey Avenue.
• **Pastries** – Everything from the Mickey donut to Mike Wazowski cranberry bread to the Mickey chocolate muffin. Sold at *Remy's Patisserie* on Mickey Avenue.
• **Mickey Ice Cream Bar** – Sold in carts park-wide.
• **Turkey Legs** – By far the park's most popular snack, with huge queues forming. Sold at *Tortuga Treats* in Treasure Cove.
• **Popcorn** – Sold park-wide from carts in a variety of flavors including steak, strawberry and caramel.

Chapter Nine | Shanghai Disneyland

Shanghai Disneyland Park Guide

Disney's largest ever Magic-Kingdom-style park is composed of seven lands filled with fantasy, adventure, and excitement.

The park is loosely based on the original Disneyland that opened in California in 1955, and the Magic Kingdom in Orlando, Florida, but with upgrades from the 21st century.

Shanghai Disneyland is the eight most visited theme park in the world. The park has plenty to offer guests with over thirty attractions (rides, themed areas, and shows), as well as character experiences, dining options, and an abundance of places to shop.

The park is divided into seven areas (or "lands") around The Enchanted Storybook Castle in the center. These are Mickey Avenue (the equivalent to Main Street USA in other Disney parks), Gardens of Imagination (the 11-acre hub area in front of the castle), Tomorrowland, Toy Story Land, Fantasyland, Treasure Cove, and Adventure Isle. Each land has its own overarching theme, with its own soundtrack, décor, costumes, and themed attractions. Unlike many other Disney Magic Kingdom-style parks, there is no Disneyland Railroad around the park to transport guests between these different lands.

We will now take a look at each land individually, as well as the attractions, dining options, and other notable features.

Waiting in queue lines is inevitable at theme parks. To help you determine how long you may wait to experience each attraction, we have included "average wait times." These averages are for peak times such as school holidays (Summer, Christmas, Golden Week) and weekends throughout the year. Wait times outside busy times are usually much lower.

	Does the attraction have Fastpass?		Minimum height (in cm)
	Is there an On-Ride Photo?		Attraction Length
	Average wait times (on peak days)		Is Disney Premier Access available?

Mickey Avenue

Mickey Avenue is the entrance to Shanghai Disneyland, taking you towards the Gardens of Imagination, Enchanted Storybook Castle and beyond. This park entrance is different in that it is shorter than all the other parks (which feature Main Street, U.S.A or a variation), and it is more cartoon-like in style. It leads to a super-hub area in front of the castle called the Gardens of Imagination.

Mickey Avenue contains shops on both sides of the street, the king of which is the Avenue M Arcade, where you are sure to find something to buy!

There are several snack locations, and one Quick Service restaurant.

Shanghai Disneyland Guest Services is immediately to your right after the turnstiles; this is the equivalent of 'City Hall' in other parks. Ask any questions you have here. They can also make reservations for tours and restaurants, and accept complaints and positive feedback too.

Registration for the Disability Access Service is available at Shanghai Disneyland Guest Services, providing easier access to attractions. See our 'Guests with Disabilities' chapter for more information on this.

You will often find character meet and greets in this area of the park, as well as live entertainment and Disney Photopass photographers.

Shanghai Disney Resort Magic Passport

The Magic Passport isn't necessarily an attraction nor is it confined to Mickey Avenue – it is a souvenir passport which you can purchase. Then you can visit different stamp stations around the park and get stamps from the machines to complete your collection.

It is a unique souvenir items that no other Disney park has.

Mickey's Film Festival at Walt Disney Grand Theatre

See a selection of short Mickey cartoon films in the beautiful Walt Disney Grand Theatre – this is a minor attraction, but a good place to go on days of inclement weather as it is rarely crowded, and out of the elements.

Dining
Chip & Dale's Treehouse Treats – Snack location. Sells nuts, popcorn, ice cream & drinks.
Remy's Patisserie – Café/snack location. Sells sandwiches, pastries, crepes, cookies, pancakes and drinks.
Il Paperino – Café/snack location. Sells waffles, ice cream and drinks.
Mickey & Pals Market Café – Quick Service. Serves stews, pork ribs, dumplings, noodles, beef steak, chicken wings and more.

Gardens of Imagination

Gardens of Imagination is a unique 11-acre super hub located between Mickey Avenue and the Enchanted Storybook Castle. This giant hub area features several attractions and gardens, and is the epicenter of the park.

As well as the attractions listed below, you can also find the following in this area of the park: the **Storyteller Statue** of Walt Disney and Mickey Mouse, and the **Melody Garden** where Chip 'n Dale perform Tai Chi in a short show.

Garden of the Twelve Friends

This is a walkthrough area, which is not really a garden but a long wall depicting the twelve signs of the Chinese zodiac with Disney characters. It makes for a great set of photo opportunities. Look out for Mushu representing the year of the dragon, Abu for the year of the monkey, and Pluto for the year of the dog.

Fantasia Carousel

This is a beautiful carousel themed to Fantasia, and is a joy to ride for every member of the family.

Whether you want to go along with the theme of Fantasia or prefer to think of it as the carousel from Mary Poppins, it is sure to be a fun-filled family adventure.

Top Tip: The carousel is least busy in the first 30 minutes of park opening and around lunchtime – otherwise it is busy right up until the closure of the park as it is usually the first attraction guests see on the way into the park, and the last one they see on the way out, as well as while waiting for the nighttime spectacular.

Note: The is no minimum height if accompanied.

FP	☆	Height	⏱	⌛
No	No	120cm	1 min 30 seconds	30 to 60 minutes

Dumbo The Flying Elephant

    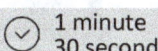

FP	☆	Height	Photo	⏱	⌛
No	No	None	No	1 minute 30 seconds	45 to 75 minutes

Dumbo is one of Disney's most popular rides for younger children. Situated to the left and in front of the *Enchanted Storybook Castle*, it offers views of the surrounding area and is a lot of fun.

In front of the seats in each flying elephant, there is a lever that allows you to lift your Dumbo up or down and fly up high!

As the ride is popular and has a low capacity, there are reasonably long waits all day from this attraction. Ride it during the parade, during Early Entry, or at the start or end of the day for the shortest waits.

Top Tip: The queue line is a decent place to watch the shows which take place on the stage in front of the Castle without battling the crowds.

Meet Mickey Tent

 No   No   None   Yes   1 to 2 mins on average   15 to 30 minutes

Admire all the portraits of Mickey and his friends in the indoor queue. Then, once you reach the front, you will enter a room with Mickey. Here you can meet the big cheese, have a chat, and get an autograph and photos.

You are welcome to take your own photos or ask the Cast Member present to help you. In addition, there is a Disney photographer there who will also take an official photo, which can be seen at the attraction's exit.

Marvel Universe

 No   No   None   Yes   Walkthrough - varies   15 to 30 minutes for characters

Marvel Universe is the place to explore adventures from the Marvel Universe. The area is made up of four main mini-attractions:
• Meet-and-greet with Captain America
• Meet-and-greet with Spider-Man
• 'Become Iron Man' where you can use screens in a video-game-style setting and your hands to simulate what it's like to be Iron Man
• Marvel Comic Academy where you can learn to draw your favorite Marvel superheroes!

There are also lots of Marvel props and photo-opportunities in this large indoor area.

There is no wait to get into Marvel Universe, only for photos with the characters.

Golden Fairytale Fanfare

This daytime show takes place in front of Enchanted Storybook Castle several times throughout the day. There is a dedicated amphitheater viewing area in front of the castle, or you can watch from the Gardens of Imagination further back, but being closer is best for this show.

The dialogue for the show is in Mandarin but the songs are in English. You can expect to see the Disney princesses and their characters such as Snow White and the Seven Dwarves, Anna and Elsa,

Aladdin and Jasmine, Ariel, Merida, and Mickey and Minnie.

The show lasts 18 minutes and you can usually get a decent spot around 15 minutes before showtime.

Dining
Timothy's Treats – Snack kiosk. Sells hot dogs, and hot and cold drinks.
Wandering Moon Restaurant – Quick Service. Serves Chinese cuisine with a huge array of choices including ribs, mackerel, crab, BBQ pork, spring rolls, roasted duck, chicken and much more. Also serves Chinese tea, soft drinks and alcohol.

Shanghai Disneyland

Disney Pixar Toy Story Land

Toy Story Land shrinks you down to the size of a toy in Andy's back yard.

Slinky Dog Spin

 No   ☆ No   None   No   ⊙ 1 minutes 30 seconds   ⏳ 45 to 60 minutes

Hop on Slinky Dog and enjoy yourself as you spin around and around in circles getting increasingly faster and faster. This is a fun family-friendly attraction that is likely to entertain everyone from young toddlers to parents.

Rex's Racer

Hop on the RC car from Toy Story, and feel the wind in your hair as you ride both forwards and backward along the track.

The ride is great fun and a good adrenaline rush – it is similar to the swinging pirate ships found at many theme parks, but we prefer the feeling on this. Here, you are also secured by overhead harnesses, which you aren't on a pirate ship.

At the highest point, riders are 24m (80ft) high, and the free-fall feeling backward is great fun.

The ride looks significantly more intimidating than it actually is and the sensation is not anywhere near as

FP No   ☆ Yes   120cm   ⊙ 1 min   ⏳ 90 to 120 minutes

scary as it seems, in our opinion.

RC Racer has one of the most boring, and tedious, queues in the park so we would recommend avoiding it if waits are long; the queue also moves very slowly.

Top Tip: Get here early to ride this attraction, as queues build up quickly, and the ride has a very low hourly guest capacity.

Woody's Roundup

 No    Yes   81cm   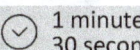 No    ⊙ 1 minute 30 seconds   ⏳ 30 to 45 minutes

Pick a pony, take a seat in a cart and get ready to spin as the music starts and the horses begin to dance. If you get dizzy easily, skip this attraction – otherwise, it is good family fun.

Dining
Toy Box Café – Snacks and Quick Service. Serves seafood, baked sweet potato, pork cutlets, pizza, pork ribs, chicken and more dishes, as well as drinks, cakes and ice cream.

Tomorrowland

Step into the land of tomorrow in the most futuristic land of any Disney theme park.

Jet Packs

Soar above Tomorrowland in your very own jet pack.

This is a spinning-type ride similar to Dumbo in Fantasyland, but the jet packs here go higher, spin faster and tilt more, making for a surprisingly good thrill.

It is a lot of fun, but it is not a must-do attraction and it is far from unique.

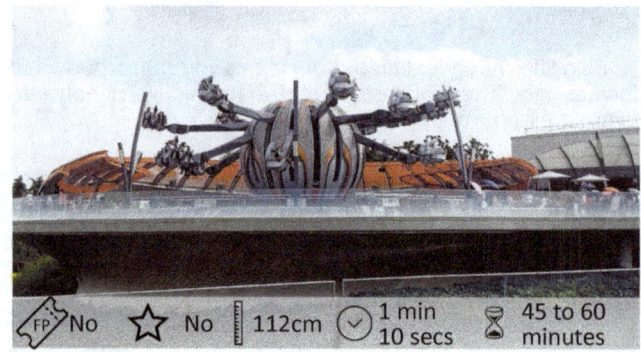

| FP: No | ★ No | 📏 112cm | ⏱ 1 min 10 secs | ⏳ 45 to 60 minutes |

Stitch Encounter

| FP: No | ★ No | 📏 None | 📷 No | ⏱ 10 minutes | ⏳ Until next show - 15 minutes |

Enter a special transmission room and before you know it, a Cast Member will connect you and your fellow earthlings in your theatre to Stitch and you will be speaking with him live in space.

Stitch is curious about how the planet Earth works, so he will ask all sorts of strange questions to learn about our home.

This attraction is good fun; however, the show is entirely in Mandarin.

Buzz Lightyear Planet Rescue

On this interactive ride, once in your Space Cruiser, you can use its laser guns to shoot at the targets, and help Buzz defeat the evil Emperor Zurg.

Different targets are worth different amounts of points and there are even hidden targets so you can score thousands of bonus points – see the queue line walls for information on which targets are worth the most!

At the end of the ride, the person with the most points wins. It is competitive, fun and endlessly re-rideable – it is also a great family adventure with no minimum height limit.

If you have visited other Disney parks, many have a similar version of this ride but this is the best version with the most accurate shooting system and more special effects.

| FP: Yes | ★ Yes | 📏 None | ⏱ 4 mins | ⏳ 20 to 30 minutes |

TRON Lightcycle Power Run

TRON Lightcycle Power Run is perhaps the most well-known attraction at Shanghai Disneyland. It takes the place of Space Mountain in the other Disney parks, and takes this experience to the next level.

On this high-speed rollercoaster, you sit forward in on a Lightcycle from the TRON franchise. This is the fastest Disney roller coaster ever built with a powerful launch at the beginning that has you hitting speeds of 95km/h (59mph). After a quick visit outside, you enter "the grid" where projections and other effects simulate a race between you and your opponents.

FP	★	↕	📷	⏱	⌛
Yes	Yes	122cm		2 mins	120 to 150 mins

Top Tip: The restraint system may be uncomfortable (and restrictive) for some guests – the best way of describing it, is being on a motorbike leaning forward travelling at high speed.

Top Tip 2: The seats for this ride are not incredibly intuitive, so when you are seated, lean forward so your legs are on the leg rests, and pull the handlebars towards you - this puts the back restraint and leg restraints in place.

TRON Realm, Chevrolet Digital Challenge

FP	★	↕	📷	⏱	⌛
No	No	None	No	Varies - Walkthrough	None

Tron Realm is a futuristic indoor interactive digital playground where guests can take part in one of three main zones:
• Create Zone: Design unique vehicles and see them come to life on screen
• Imagine Zone: See what the future of vehicles could look like such as automated driving and parking
• Drive Zone: This driving simulator area lets you take cool vehicles for a spin

Located right beside the main *TRON Lightcycle Power Run* attraction, this is a good place for any non-riders to spend some time.

Star Wars Launch Bay

Star Wars Launch Bay is an indoor walkthrough area similar to *Marvel Universe* in Gardens of Imagination.

Here you will find character meet-and-greets such as Storm Troopers, C3PO and R2D2, Kylo Ren, and more.

There is a screening room with a highlight reel of the Star Wars movies.

Plus, there are plenty of photo opportunities including the cockpit of the Millennium Falcon, Stormtrooper helmets, and lightsabers. Star Wars fans will geek out!

Dining
Spiral Snacks – Snack location. Serves ice cream, jumbo spring rolls, and duck and cheese buns, as well as hot and cold drinks.
Stargazer Grill – Quick Service. Serves mainly Western cuisine such as burgers and fried chicken. Also serves drinks and ice cream.

Fantasyland

Find classic Disney attractions here, in this land dedicated to the youngest members of the family, as well as several new additions that are unique to Shanghai Disneyland.

In addition to the attractions listed on the following pages, Fantasyland also contains **Festival Forest** where you can try to pull out the Sword in The Stone and watch short live shows.

Enchanted Storybook Castle

Standing 60m (200ft) tall, the *Enchanted Storybook Castle*, is the centerpiece and icon of Shanghai Disneyland Park. It is both the tallest and widest Disney castle ever created.

When the Imagineers were designing Shanghai Disneyland, they knew that the castle here had to be different and unlike the castles in the American Disney theme parks – instead of just representing once princess such as Sleeping Beauty or Cinderella, this castle was designed to represent all the Disney princesses. The attention to detail is stunning.

The castle is not just for show, however, and can actually be explored by guests – it contains the park's only Table Service restaurant (**Royal Banquet Hall**), a princess make-over experience called **'Bibbidi Bobbidi Boutique'**, **Storybook Court** (a princess meet and greet) and a walkthrough attraction – **"Once Upon a Time" Adventure**. On the ground floor, you can walk through the main atrium and enjoy this magical building from the inside. The castle is also the backdrop to shows which are performed at the stage in front.

The Many Adventures of Winnie the Pooh

 Yes   Yes   None   No   3 minutes   45 to 75 minutes

Hop inside one of Pooh's "hunny pots" and explore one of his many adventures.

This is a gentle ride where you venture through Pooh's stories; it includes slight rocking and jumping motions to enhance the experience.

As well as the popular characters, the ride is filled with bright colors that should excite the little ones.

This is a clone of the attractions at Disneyland and Walt Disney World, so if you have ridden those you may consider skipping this.

"Once Upon a Time" Adventure

Step into the Enchanted Storybook Castle and enjoy the magic of Disney fairytales come to life before your very eyes as special effects bring the storybooks to life.

Next, enter the beautiful atrium and ascend the stairs as you go past beautiful photo opportunities with carvings of all the Disney princesses.

Once upstairs you will see the story of Snow White retold in short scenes using 3D and 4D effects. The attraction audio is entirely in Mandarin, but it is worth everyone experiencing and

FP: No | No | None | 20 mins | 5 to 15 mins

you are not really missing out on anything as the story is easy to follow.

At the end of the experience you are rewarded with a beautiful hidden garden nested among the rooftops of the castle.

Peter Pan's Flight

Peter Pan's Flight features beloved characters, it is family-friendly and provides a small thrill too.

Hop aboard a flying pirate ship and take a voyage through the world of Peter Pan and Never Never Land. As you soar, you will see scenes to the sides and underneath you, in a retelling of the classic story. If you have been to the other Disney parks, this is a very similar experience but on a grander scale and with more modern effects.

The ride's interior is stunning from the moment you step inside.

This can be a popular ride, but waits do ease during the day compared to something like *Seven Dwarves Mine*

FP: Yes | Yes | None | 4 mins | 60 to 75 mins

Train, so we do not necessarily recommend using a Fastpass for this ride.

Important: Visitors who are afraid of heights may find this ride unsuitable. The ships you sit in give the sensation of flight, and at times you will be several meters off the ground and descending steeply (albeit not too quickly). These sensations may surprise some guests — mostly, though, it seems to be adults who are affected by this, and not children.

Voyage to the Crystal Grotto

Voyage to the Crystal Grotto is a unique ride to Shanghai Disneyland in which you set sail aboard boats through Fantasyland in this gentle ride. As you round each corner you will see statues of popular Disney movies, including Mulan and Beauty and the Beast, come to life with music and fountains.

As you near the journey's end a stunning surprise awaits you as you glide along the waterway inside the castle and the rockwork comes to life with Disney classics.

This attraction has one of

FP: No | ☆ Yes | None | ⊙ 11 mins | ⧗ 30 to 45 mins

the more tedious queue lines in the park with no real theming, so try to visit early in the day to skip any significant waits. *Voyage to the Crystal Grotto* closes a few hours before the rest of the park to prepare for the nighttime spectacular on the castle.

Hunny Pot Spin

Hop inside one of Pooh's 'hunny pots' and go for a wild spin, but watch out for the bees overhead!

The ride functions much like any other teacup ride around the world, where you have a wheel at the center of the cup that you can turn to spin yourself around faster. Or, leave it alone and have a more relaxing spin.

FP: No | ☆ No | None | ⊙ 1 min 30 secs | ⧗ 15 to 30 mins

Frozen: A Sing-Along Celebration at Evergreen Playhouse

Show Length: 20 minutes

Watch a retelling of the "Frozen" story. As the show evolves, the show becomes a sing-a-long every time a song comes on. This show now features scenes and songs from Frozen 2 too!

The show culminates with the arrival of Elsa, making for a stunning finale.

This show is entirely in Mandarin, including all the songs.

Seven Dwarfs Mine Train

This fun roller coaster contains both inside dark ride elements and outside roller coaster sections taking you into the world of Snow White and the Seven Dwarf's mine where "a million diamonds shine".

The ride cars are unique in that they swing as guests go around bends as real mine carts would.

The thrill level is well below *TRON*, the other coaster in the park; this is definitely more of a family ride.

Seven Dwarfs Mine Train ride has a Single Rider line, which can prove useful when there are long waits – this is pretty much all the time and this ride competes for the longest queue line in the whole park with *Soaring*.

This is a clone of the attraction at Walt Disney World, so if you have ridden it there you may wish to consider skipping this to make the most of your time in the park. This version does not have an interactive queue line and the songs are in Mandarin, and there are some very minor scene changes.

FP: Yes | ★ Yes | 97cm | 3 mins | 150 to 180 mins

Alice in Wonderland Maze

Hop inside one of Pooh's 'hunny pots' and go for a wild spin, but watch out for the bees overhead!

The ride functions much like any other teacup ride around the world, where you have a wheel at the center of the cup that you can turn to spin yourself around faster. Or, leave it alone and have a more relaxing spin.

FP: No | ★ No | None | 5 to 10 mins | None

Dining

Royal Banquet Hall – Table Service with Disney characters. Serves Chinese & Western dishes in a 3-course meal. Entrees include lobster tail, pork belly, beef short-rib & vegetable curry.
Pinocchio Village Kitchen – Quick Service. Serves rice bowls, noodles, pizzas and drinks.
Fairy Godmother's Cupboard – Snack location. Serves bento combos, pizza & ice creams.
Troubadour Treats – Snack location. Serves bento combos, hot and cold drinks, sweet egg tarts and ice creams.
Tangled Tree Tavern – Quick Service. Serves roast chicken, beef, crispy pork, curry rice, seafood, and vegetables with sweet and sour sauce.
Merlin's Magic Recipe – Snack location. Serves Chinese cuisine such as bento combos, sweet egg tarts, sausage rolls, lemon mousse cake, and hot and cold drinks.
You will also find a popcorn cart, and a pretzel and churros cart in Fantasyland.

Treasure Cove

Treasure Cove is the first Disney theme park land themed entirely to pirates. Although the whole park is beautiful, the attention to detail here is extraordinary, making Treasure Cove our favorite part of the resort.

Pirates of the Caribbean: Battle for the Sunken Treasure

| FP: No | Yes | None | Photo: Yes | 10 minutes | 30 to 45 minutes |

Pirates of the Caribbean: Battle for the Sunken Treasure is perhaps the most immersive and technologically advanced ride in the whole of China – this attraction set a new benchmark for Disney and really needs to be seen to be believed.

If you have visited a Disney theme park before, you will almost certainly have ridden Pirates of the Caribbean – this attraction is completely unique, however. The storyline is based on the movies, and the interior of the attraction is entirely different.

Battle for the Sunken Treasure fuses real-life props with screens, incredible audio-animatronics, water effects and some clever Disney magic to make a ride that puts you in the middle of a contentious battle. Overall – this is a must-do!

There is a Single Rider queue line available for this attraction which moves incredibly quickly and will save you a lot of time during busy parts of the day.

The middle of the day is the busiest for this attraction. You can typically ride with a minimal wait of 15 minutes or less in the last 90 minutes of park operation.

Shripwreck Shore

Shipwreck Shore is a giant interactive play area, featuring water features, water guns, bridges, a shipwreck, lookout points and plenty of photo opportunities.

This area is open to everyone of all ages and is not just limited to children – you may well get wet here, making it a great place to cool off on warmer days.

Siren's Revenge

This is a walkthrough area where you can step aboard a pirate ship and explore all the little details – the ship does not move. This is a good place for photos with the *Enchanted Storybook Castle* in the background.

Explorer Canoes

If you fancy a bit of exercise and a really unique and detailed view of Treasure Cove from all its angles, then this is the perfect attraction for you – here, you provide the power as you use a real canoe to sail around the island.

With twenty of you powering at the same time, it is less effort than it might appear – an interesting and unique theme park experience.

Top Tip: This attraction closes before sunset.

FP No · No · See below · 10 mins · 45 to 60 mins

Minimum Height: Feet must touch the floor when seated.

Eye of the Storm – Captain Jack's Stunt Spectacular at El Teatro Fandango

'Eye of the Storm' is a live show featuring Jack Sparrow and a bunch of his pirate friends (and enemies). The show is performed entirely in Mandarin but this is a stunt show – and it is the stunts you are here to see! There is a particularly impressive moment when the Eye of the Storm arrives inside the theater!

The pre-show, in particular, is loud with several gunshots so this may not be suitable for very young members of the family or those startled by loud noises.

FP No · No · None · 30 mins · Until next show

Dining
The Snackin' Kraken – Snack location. Serves pork floss buns and Minnie chocolate donuts, as well as hot and cold drinks.
Barbossa's Bounty – Quick Service inside the *Pirates of the Caribbean* building – see other guests sail by as you eat. Serves chicken, beef, duck, lamb, BBQ ribs, red fish and vegetable patties.
Pintel & Ragetti's Grub to Grab – Snack location. Sells hot dogs and drinks.
Tortuga Treats – Snack location. Sells turkey legs, ice creams and drinks – very popular with big crowds.

There is also a popcorn cart in this area.

Adventure Isle

According to the Disney legend, Adventure Isle is based around the League of Adventurers, an explorer group who set up camp in this area in 1935. These adventurers now welcome other explorers like you to the area.

As well as the attractions covered on the following pages, you will find a character meet-and-greet location called **Happy Circle** in Adventure Isle, as well as the **Storyhouse Stage** (which at the time of writing is not presenting any shows but has featured Tarzan in the past).

Soaring Over the Horizon

 Yes   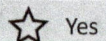 Yes   102cm   No   15 mins (incl. pre-show)   150 to 180 minutes

Shanghai Disneyland's most popular attraction, *Soaring Over the Horizon* gives you the chance to experience what it is like to fly and hang glide over places around the world.

It is a truly immersive experience with smells and slow movement to match a giant on-screen video, creating an incredibly realistic sensation of flight. The Chinese audience loves this ride and you will hear a lot of gasps and wows as you fly. If you are scared of heights this ride is most definitely not for you.

For us, this is one of the best attractions in the whole park - the concept is simple but the execution is excellent. It is, however, exactly the same film as the other *Soaring* rides in the Disney resorts in Tokyo and in the US (barring the last scene - the pre-show and queue theming are different), so given the very long wait times, if you are short on time, you may wish to skip it.

Roaring Rapids

This fun group water ride starts off as a serene journey and soon turns into an encounter with a gigantic mythical beast and a couple of drops down waterfalls.

This ride makes sure that everyone gets at least a little bit wet - however, one or two people will come out soaked.

This attraction is particularly popular on hot summer days towards the middle of the day. We recommend making a Fastpass reservation as the queue line is slow-moving.

Yes   Yes   107cm   7 mins   60 to 90 mins

Camp Discovery

Camp Discovery is the centerpiece of Adventure Isle and is based around a mountain. The main attraction here is *Challenge Trails* (which is covered below), but you can also explore the mountain and surroundings on foot in *Vista Trail*, and visit the *Excavation Site* playground for kids.

Challenge Trails at Camp Discovery

Challenge Trails is a unique ropes course that cannot be found at any other Disney park. Once you have your harness on and you are securely fastened onto the ropes course line by a Cast Member, you are free to explore one of three ropes courses – on each course, there are a number of obstacles and when you get to each obstacle you can choose one of three ways to defeat that obstacle from easy to hard.

Obstacles include swinging barrels, rope bridges, squeezing by the side of a waterfall and much more – there are some genuinely scary moments if you opt for the tougher level. This truly is one of our favorite attractions in the park as it really feels like you are on an adventure and nowhere near a theme park.

FP No ☆ Yes ▯ 106cm ⊘ 15 to 20 mins ⧗ 60 to 75 mins

You will put *all* your items (including your smartphone) in a free locker before entering the main queue line – at peak times, there can be a long wait even to deposit your items. You will also need to wear closed toe shoes (no sandals or fli-flops) – we also recommend ladies do not wear skirts!

This attraction usually opens about 1 hour after the rest of the park, so be there about 10-15 minutes before this as a queue will form. The wait times do get reasonably high for this attraction very quickly due to the low capacity. Also, bare in mind it also closes earlier than the rest of the park.

Dining
Piranha Bites – Snack location. Serves beef & chicken wraps, as well as hot & cold drinks.
Tribal Table – Quick Service. Serves turkey legs, chicken, eggplant & tacos, and drinks.

There is also a popcorn cart and a corndog cart in this area.

Park Entertainment

Ignite the Dream, A Nighttime Spectacular of Magic and Light

Disney theme parks around the world are renowned for ending visitors' days by lighting up the sky with incredible firework displays. Shanghai Disneyland is no exception.

Ignite the Dream is Shanghai Disneyland's dazzling nighttime spectacular which coordinates music, projections, lasers, water fountains and fireworks.

You can expect to see scenes from movies such as Star Wars, Frozen, Pirates of the Caribbean, The Little Mermaid, The Lion King and Finding Nemo.

Ignite the Dream is performed nightly at the closing of Disneyland Park. The show runs for 19 minutes. After the fireworks, Mickey Avenue's shops remain open for a short period for your shopping convenience.

Ignite the Dream is primarily a projection show that relies heavily on you having a view of the front of the *Enchanted Storybook Castle*. Although the fireworks can be seen from across the park, you will not see key parts of the show if you are not viewing the front of the castle and its projections. The front is also where the lasers, fountains and fire effects can be seen.

You will want to position yourself in the Gardens of Imagination (hub) area of the park for the best view. Due to the enormity of the hub, we would advise you to not be too far back as you can easily feel distant from the castle, despite its size.

We recommend staking out a spot about 1 hour 30 minutes before the show is set to begin – the hub area in front of the castle can accommodate a large number of people, but Cast Members begin to close off areas as they fill up. There is also a lot of clutter in this area of the park which limits sightlines to the castle – this includes trees, lampposts, statues and even the *Carousel* and *Dumbo* attractions.

Find a spot with a railing in front of you – this prevents someone from turning up during the show and obscuring your view. This often happens when guests put their children on their shoulders as the show begins, ruining the view for everyone behind. Equally frustrating is someone filming the show on their phone blocking your view.

Mickey's Storybook Express

Parade Length: 15 minutes

Mickey's Storybook Express is the best way to see all your favourite Disney characters in one place as they parade through Toy Story Land, Tomorrowland and around the Gardens of Imagination.

The parade is performed daily and the time varies seasonally – during times of peak attendance, the parade is performed twice. Check the app or Times Guide for the exact schedule.

Characters in the parade may vary from day to day but you can typically see about 50 different characters and floats, including: Pluto, Daisy, Donald, Mickey, Chip 'n Dale, the Seven Dwarves, Lotso, Jessie, the Green Army Men, Buzz, Woody, Rapunzel and Flynn, characters from Finding Dory, Olaf, Anna and Elsa, Mulan, Winnie the Pooh, Tigger, Eeyore, characters from Zootopia, Stitch, Captain Hook, Pinocchio, Duffy and many more.

It is not just the characters that are exciting though, the

floats are amazing too. The soundtrack is a mix of English and Mandarin.

The most popular place to watch the parade is from Gardens of Imagination. You should secure your spot about 20 to 30 minutes before the parade starts for the best view if watching from here.

The parade is not canceled during light or moderate rain. During heavy rain, or if there is a thunderstorm alert, there is the potential for the parade to be canceled or delayed. In either case, an announcement will be made at the parade start time.

Top Tip: If you are familiar with the parade route from other Disney parks, do check the park map as this one differs greatly.

Top Tip 2: We find that the crowds get very pushy during the parade, so a good idea is to stand next to a lamppost by the parade route so no-one can squeeze in that space or put an umbrella up blocking your view!

Top Tip 3: If watching the parade from Gardens of Imagination, try to be on the outside of the circle so you can get better photos as the floats and characters approach.

Chapter Ten | Touring Plans

Touring Plans

Touring plans are easy-to-follow guides that minimize your waiting time in queue lines throughout the day. By following them, you can maximize your time in the parks and experience more attractions. There are several different touring plans available to suit your needs.

To see all of Shanghai Disneyland, you will need to allocate two days. However, you can hit the headline attractions at the park in just one day if you are pressed for time.

These touring plans are not set in stone, so feel free to adapt them to the needs of your party. It is important to note that these plans focus on experiencing the rides; if your focus is on meeting all the characters or seeing all the shows, then a touring plan is unlikely to be suitable for you. The only way to minimize waits for characters is to get to the parks and the meet-and-greets early.

These touring plans are intense, BUT you will get to cram in as much as possible during your visit. If you are at the resort for multiple days, feel free to follow the plans at a more leisurely pace. Also, if you do not want to experience a particular ride, skip that step but do not change the order of the steps.

If an attraction is closed for refurbishment during your trip, skip those steps.

You must purchase your tickets in advance to make the most of your time and these touring plans. If you need to buy a ticket on the day, turn up 1 hour earlier than the recommended start times on these plans - and even earlier during peak season.

Insider Tip: To minimize the time you spend waiting in queue lines, you will often need to cross the park from one side to the other – this is purposely done by theme parks to disperse crowds more evenly. Note, for example, how the most popular attractions at Shanghai Disneyland are all in different lands and far away from each other.

1 Day Plan for Guests with Early Entry

Step 1: Be at the park entry turnstiles 15 minutes before the start of Early Entry. Pick up a Park Map and a Times Guide, which lists parade, show, character and firework times, as well as attraction closures (you can also use the app for this).

Step 2: Link your park tickets to your Shanghai Disney Resort app and book a Fastpass for *Soaring Over the Horizon*.

Step 3: Head to *TRON Lightcycle Power Run*. Ride it.

Step 4: Go to *Seven Dwarves Mine Train*. Ride it.

Use Single Rider if the wait is longer than 20 minutes.

Step 5: Check the app to see what time the *Challenge Trails* at *Camp Discovery* open. This attraction usually opens 1 hour after the rest of the park, but not always. You will want to be waiting outside the entrance to *Camp Discovery* about 10 to

Touring Plans

15 minutes before it opens. So, if you have at least 45 minutes left until then, explore the Treasure Cove area of the park or *Alice in Wonderland Maze* on the way to *Camp Discovery*. If there are less than 45 minutes left, head to *Camp Discovery* now.

Step 6: Store your belongings in one of the provided lockers and enjoy one of the *Challenge Trails at Camp Discovery*.

Step 7: You should now be eligible to get another Fastpass. Use this for *Roaring Rapids*. If that is not available, then use it for *Peter Pan's Flight*.

Step 8: Remember to use your *Soaring* Fastpass when that comes up too.

Step 9: Go to *Voyage to the Crystal Grotto*. Ride it.

Step 10: Have an early lunch.

Step 11: Between 1:00pm and 5:00pm is usually the busiest time of the day at the theme park so this is a good time to explore

attractions that usually have a constant wait time or to watch shows. Head to Tomorrowland. Explore *Star Wars Launch Bay, TRON Realm*, and ride *Buzz Lightyear Planet Rescue*.

Step 12: Head to Fantasyland and experience "*Once Upon a Time Adventure*".

Step 13: Is it parade time yet? If so, get a spot for *Mickey's Storybook Express*.

Step 14: Be sure to use your *Soaring* and *Roaring Rapids* or *Peter Pan's Flight* Fastpasses. Work these around the rest of the plan.

Step 15: Check the performance schedule of *Eye of the Storm* and work this around a ride on *Pirates of the Caribbean*. Do these back-to-back. Use Single Rider at *Pirates* if the wait is longer than 20 minutes.

Step 16: You have now done most of the park's main rides – use the next couple of hours to explore Fantasyland and ride *The Many Adventures of Winnie the Pooh, Peter Pan's Flight*

if you have not done so already, and perhaps even watch *Frozen: A Sing-Along Celebration*. Have a snack too!

Step 17: You can also explore Toy Story Land's three rides – all get very high wait times for what are fairly standard fairground-style attractions.

Step 18: Squeeze in a ride on *TRON Lightcycle Power Run* when it gets dark – this ride is even better at nighttime.

Step 19: Check when the night-time show *Ignite the Dream* is being presented. This should not be missed! Now depending on what time of the day it is, and when the park closes, it is either time to watch *Ignite the Dream* or have dinner.

Step 20: Get a spot in front of the castle in *Gardens of Imagination* at least 1 hour 30 minutes before *Ignite the Dream* begins. We grab a waffle from *Il Paperino* while waiting to help the time pass. If you don't want a perfect view, then feel free to arrive 30 minutes before the show begins.

1 Day Plan for Guests without Early Entry

This plan relies on you using Single Rider every time when it is available.

Step 1: Be at the park entry turnstiles 30 minutes before the scheduled opening of the park. Pick up a Park Map and a Times Guide (you can also use the app for this).

Step 2: Link your park tickets to your Shanghai Disney Resort app and book a Fastpass for *Soaring Over the Horizon*.

Step 3: Head to *Seven Dwarves Mine Train*. Ride it using Single Rider.

Step 4: Check the app to see what time the Challenge Trails at Camp Discovery open. This attraction usually opens 1 hour after the rest of the park, but not always. Be outside the entrance to *Camp Discovery* 10 to 15 minutes before it opens. Head there now.

Step 5: Store your belongings in one of the provided lockers and enjoy one of the *Challenge Trails at Camp Discovery*.

Step 6: Go to *TRON Lightcycle Power Run*. Ride it using Single Rider.

Step 7: You should now be eligible for another Fastpass – you can book this while waiting for *TRON*. Use this Fastpass for *Roaring Rapids*. If that is not available, then use it for *Peter Pan's Flight*.

Step 8: Remember to use your *Soaring* Fastpass when that comes up too.

Step 9: Have an early lunch.

Step 10: Head to Fantasyland and ride *Voyage to the Crystal Grotto*.

Step 11: 1:00pm to 5:00pm is usually the busiest time of the day at the park, so this is a good time to explore attractions that have a constant wait time or to watch shows. Experience *"Once Upon a Time Adventure"*.

Step 12: Is it parade time yet? If so, get a spot for *Mickey's Storybook Express*. If not, visit *Alice in Wonderland Maze* in the meantime.

Step 13: Work your *Soaring* and *Roaring Rapids* or *Peter Pan's Flight* Fastpasses around the rest of the plan.

Step 14: Check the performance schedule of *Eye of the Storm* and work this around riding *Pirates of the Caribbean*. Do these back-to-back. Use Single Rider at *Pirates* if the wait is longer than 20 minutes.

Step 15: You have now done most of the park's main rides – use the next couple of hours to explore Fantasyland and ride *The Many Adventures of Winnie the Pooh*, *Peter Pan's Flight* if you have not done so already, and perhaps even watch *Frozen: A Sing-Along Celebration*. Grab a snack!

Step 16: You can also explore Toy Story Land's three rides – all get very high wait times for what are fairly standard fairground-style attractions.

Step 17: Experience *TRON Lightcycle Power Run* when it gets dark – this ride is even better at nighttime.

Step 18: Check when *Ignite the Dream* is being presented. This should not be missed! Now, it is either time to watch *Ignite the Dream* or have dinner.

Step 19: Get a spot in front of the castle in Gardens of Imagination at least 1 hour 30 minutes before Ignite the Dream begins. We grab a waffle from *Il Paperino* while waiting. If you don't want a perfect view, then arrive 30 minutes before the show begins.

2-Day Plan

This plan is looser as you have a lot more free time. The most important part of the plan is the first hour of each morning. This plan is in note-form.

As you can see you can very easily experience everything in the park with only minimal waits when you have two days to visit the resort.

Day 1
Morning:
• Be at the turnstiles 15-30 minutes before you can enter the park.
• Get a *Soaring Over the Horizon* Fastpass.
• Ride *Seven Dwarves Mine Train*.
• Get in the queue for *Challenge Trails at Camp Discovery* 15 minutes before this opens. Experience the *Challenge Trails*.
• Ride *Roaring Rapids*. Get a Fastpass for *The Many Adventures of Winnie the Pooh*.
• Watch *Eye of the Storm*.
• Ride *Pirates of the Caribbean*.
• Explore the rest of Treasure Cove's walkthrough areas.
• Have lunch at *Royal Banquet Hall*.

Afternoon:
• Experience *"Once Upon a Time Adventure"*
• Watch *Mickey's Storybook Express*

• Watch *Golden Fairytale Fanfare*
• Ride *Hunny Pot Spin* and *The Many Adventures of Winnie the Pooh* (with Fastpass).
• Grab a snack

Evening:
• Watch *Frozen: A Sing-Along Celebration*
• Ride *TRON Lightcycle Power Run* at night (use Single Rider if there is a long wait)
• Have dinner
• Grab a spot for *Ignite the Dream* at least 90 minutes before showtime (or up to 30 minutes before for a non-perfecr view)

Day 2
Morning:
• Be at the turnstiles 15-30 minutes before you can enter the park.
• Get a *TRON Lightcycle Power Run* Fastpass.
• Ride the three rides in Toy Story Land: *Rex's Racer,* then *Slinky Dog Spin,* then *Woody's Roundup*.
• Ride *Voyage to the Crystal Grotto*.
• Use your *TRON Lightcycle Power Run* Fastpass
• Get a *Peter Pan's Flight* Fastpass
• Ride *Buzz Lightyear Planet Rescue*

Afternoon:
• Explore *Star Wars Launch Bay*
• See *Marvel Universe* and meet the characters
• Meet *Mickey Mouse*
• Ride *Peter Pan's Flight* using your Fastpass

Evening:
• Re-do any favorite rides, use Single Rider queues to reduce your waits further.

Outside the Theme Park

Disneytown

Disneytown is a shopping, dining and entertainment district located just next to the theme park and on-site hotels.

The area is open even after the parks close, or you can grab lunch from here. Disneytown houses a live stage show, restaurants, shops, and more.

Admission to Disneytown is free and no ticket is required.

Disneytown Dining

Your dining options at Disneytown are:
- **blue frog bar & grill**: Western casual dining restaurant & bar
- **BreadTalk**: International boutique bakery
- **Crystal Jade**: Authentic modern Cantonese cuisine
- **DONDONYA**: Japanese donburi rice bowl restaurant
- **Food Republic**: Casual dining food hall
- **g+ The Urban**
- **Harvest**: Contemporary western restaurant offering healthy dining
- **Hatsune**: Contemporary Japanese cuisine
- **HEYTEA**: Popular tea store
- **IPPUDO**: Japanese ramen noodle restaurant
- **KOKIO Gastrobar**: Trendy bar and bistro
- **Lost Heaven**: Authentic taste of South West China
- **Molokai**: Creative Hong Kong-style bistro
- **Shanghai Min**: Authentic Shanghainese cuisine
- **Starbucks Coffee**: Coffee shop
- **The Cheesecake Factory**: Casual international cuisine
- **The Dining Room**: Shanghainese cuisine and dim sum
- **Wolfgang Puck Kitchen + Bar**: Contemporary American classics
- **Xin Wang**: Cantonese tea house restaurant

Beauty and the Beast – The Musical

The beautiful 1200-seat Walt Disney Grand Theatre in Disneytown hosts a Broadway-style stage version of Beauty and the Beast. If you are a fan of the movie, then this show is a must-see.

There are over 80 performers and crew who put on the show, with beautiful costumes, music and sets.

The show is presented entirely in Mandarin (there is no English version or subtitling), and you can buy tickets in advance from batb.shanghaidisneyresort.com/en/ or from Klook.com.

Disneytown Shopping

There are also a variety of shops at Disneytown.

- **adidas**: Sporting goods, lifestyle apparel and footwear
- **BAPE STORE**: Premium adult and kids' streetwear
- **Build-A-Bear**: Make your own stuffed animal
- **CHINA POST**: China Post sells custom exclusive gifts
- **D-Street**: Sells Disney apparel, accessories and personalized tech products that fuse street flair with the spirit of Disney
- **Hot Toys**: High-end Marvel and Star Wars collectibles
- **i.t**: Multi-brand fashion apparel and accessories
- **ICBC**: Bank services and precious metals
- **innisfree**: Korean natural cosmetics
- **LEGO**: The largest LEGO flagship store in the world
- **Masquerade by Arribas**: Face painting and merchandise
- **Nike Disneytown Door**: Sporting footwear and apparel for people of all ages
- **Novel-D**: Novelty and lifestyle Disney products
- **PANDORA**: Contemporary jewelry brand
- **SEPHORA**: Skincare, cosmetics and fragrance
- **SHEL'TTER**: Young fashion apparel
- **Superdry**: British premium fashion brand of apparel and accessories
- **Swatch**: Swiss-made fashion watches
- **SKECHERS**: Popular international performance and lifestyle footwear
- **Tren-D**: Trendy apparel with Disney character!
- **UGG**: Fashion boots, slippers and shoes
- **World of Disney**: From floor to ceiling, you'll be surrounded by all things Disney: apparel, accessories, jewelry, technology, toys, collectibles, pins, plush... the list goes on!

Wishing Star Park

Wishing Star Park is a large lake and park located just outside of Shanghai Disneyland between the theme park, Disneytown and Shanghai Disneyland Hotel.

In all honesty, despite Disney's marketing, there is no major reason for you to explore the lake at the moment, although there is a 2.5km walk around the lake where you can see woodland, flowers, marshes and maybe even some wildlife. There is also a playground, and boats cross the lake to and from the Shanghai Disneyland Hotel.

The Shanghai Disney Resort is only 4 years old in 2020, and we expect the lake to have more of a purpose in the coming years – as the resort grows with more theme parks and hotels, the lake will likely form the centerpiece of the resort.

Shanghai Village (Shopping Outlet)

Shanghai Village is a luxury shopping outlet destination located on the far end of Wishing Star Lake from Shanghai Disneyland. You can walk from the theme park or Shanghai Disneyland Hotel in about 20-25 minutes along the serene shores of the lake, or you can catch a shuttle bus (by exit 4 for shuttle bus 1 to Qimiao Road) from Shanghai Disney metro station for ¥1 and be at the outlet in about 5 minutes.

As well as various places to eat, you can expect to find over 150 brands such as Adidas, Armani Outlet, Burberry, Calvin Klein, Converse, Coach, Diesel, Gucci, Givenchy, Hugo Boss, Jack Wolfskin, Kate Spade, Lacoste, Lulu Lemon, Levi's, Mulberry, Michael Kors, Moschino, Nike, Polo Ralph Lauren, Patagonia, Samsonite, Swarovski, The North Face, Timberland, UGG, Versace and many more.

Chapter Twelve | Guests with Disabilities

Guests with Disabilities

This section covers procedures and accommodations Disney makes for guests visiting with disabilities. It includes people with mobility, hearing and visual impairments, and the Disability Access Service for the theme park. Shanghai Disney Resort calls its aim to include all guests in the fun 'Magic ALL'.

Mobility

Shanghai Disney Resort strives to allow all guests to utilize the main attraction entrances whenever possible, allowing the ride queuing system to be as fair as possible for all guests, whatever their physical or mental abilities. All park toilets are accessible too.

However, accessibility does vary from attraction to attraction within the Disney Parks – disabled guests should ask a Cast Member at the entrance to an attraction for the appropriate entrance. Sometimes guests can ride in their own wheelchairs; other times, they must transfer to a park wheelchair, and other times they must transfer to a ride vehicle.

To rent a wheelchair, proceed to the stroller rental locations near the main entrance of each of the two theme parks. Guests may also bring their own wheelchair into the parks.

Pricing is ¥90 per day for a wheelchair rental from the park.

All Shanghai Disney Resort transportation accommodates wheelchairs.

Hearing

Guests with hearing disabilities have access to Assistive Listening Systems which use a receiver to amplify sound and are recommended for guests with mild to moderate hearing loss.

This service is available at: *Frozen Sing-Along Celebration*, *Eye of the Storm: Captain Jack's Stunt Spectacular*, *Soaring Over the Horizon*, *Stitch Encounter* and *Buzz Lightyear Planet Rescue*.

Receivers, headphones and induction loops are available at Guest Services near the Main Entrance to Shanghai Disneyland, and at Walt Disney Grand Theatre in Disneytown. A refundable deposit is required.

Visual

Guests with visual disabilities have the following accommodations for them at the theme parks: Braille guidebooks, and stationary tactile maps. The maps are available in both English and Simplified Chinese.

At the Resort Hotels

Examples of accommodations that are offered in resort hotels include wheelchair-accessible bathrooms, wider bathroom doors, emergency call buttons, and ramps and elevators. We recommend calling the Shanghai Disney Resort on +86 400 180 0000 to discuss requirements in more detail.

Disability Access Service (DAS)

The Disability Access Service (DAS) is designed to assist guests with disabilities (including non-apparent disabilities) that are not able to wait in a normal queue line – their privileges will also extend to their party.

The DAS system can be activated from Guest Relations at each theme park. We recommend having some proof of disability with you. Having a translation in Simplified Chinese is not required but will likely help.

At Guest Relations, the guests will have their photo taken and information regarding the number of guests in the party is recorded. This information is linked to the theme park ticket for the disabled guest.

How does the system work?
A disabled guest goes to an attraction, or character meet, and asks the Cast Member there to use the DAS – the ride attendant will issue the guest with a ride entry time (this will be roughly the same wait time as the current standby wait time). E.g., it is 2:00 pm and the wait time for an attraction is 45 minutes – the guest is issued with a 2:45 pm return time.

The guest and their party will be able to wait in a separate area, along with their party, instead of in the queue until the designated time (guests may not be able to experience the shows or presentations in the queue area). Guests will not be able to experience another attraction or Disney Character greeting while using this service. This service is not intended to shorten guests' wait time at an attraction or a Disney Character greeting location, but to prevent the need to queue.

Depending on the degree of assistance needed or specific conditions at an attraction, DAS guests' wait time may be longer than that of the Guests standing in the standby line.

The system can be combined with Fastpass, and guests will still get full Fastpass entitlements, in addition to being able to use the system.

Shanghai Disneyland for Disney Park Veterans

Many guests visit Shanghai Disneyland after having visited the Walt Disney World Resort in Florida or the Disneyland Resort in California. All three resorts immerse you in the Disney magic, but the locations are all very different. This chapter helps you compare and contrast.

Local Customs

In this respect, the Disneyland Resort and Shanghai Disney Resorts are most alike – both these resorts have tourists, but primarily cater to a local, national audience. They are unlike Walt Disney World's visitors from all corners of the world (but mainly Americans).

In terms of theme park etiquette, guests at Shanghai Disneyland do not have the same concept of 'personal space' as in the West. Particularly around characters, in queue lines, and during parades which can become pushy.

Expect to see queue jumping in the park too, as well as a lot of umbrellas blocking your view of shows or parades with no regard for the people behind them watching.

You can also expect to see many guests bringing their own food into the park – although this was previously forbidden, Shanghai Disneyland has now relented. This can be for monetary reasons as well as cultural.

Finally, tipping is also different. Table Service meals at the resort have a

service charge included in the price of 15% - there is no need to tip on top of this.

The Cast Members and Languages

The Cast Members in Florida and California, for the most part, go above and beyond, are incredibly polite, are never rude to a guest, have a passion for Disney and do everything to make your stay as magical as possible.

We also have the same impression of Shanghai Disneyland despite the language barrier – the vast majority of Cast Members are extremely helpful and smiley (perhaps even more than in the US), but the lack of English does mean they cannot help you as much.

There does not seem to be a requirement of speaking English to work at the resort, which is understandable as the majority of the park's guests are Chinese. If you have visited Disney theme parks before, then you will be familiar with how most things work at the resort anyway such as Fastpass and Single Rider and will have very little interaction with Cast Members outside of hello, goodbye and ordering food, so the language barrier shouldn't be an issue.

When ordering food, you will see photos of the different meals and can order by pointing. Each shop or restaurant seems to have at least one person who speaks good English who is called upon if another Cast Member cannot understand you.

Hotel reception staff and Guest Relations staff seem to have the strongest level of English.

If you can, learn a few Mandarin phrases – it is very much appreciated.

Resort Size and Transportation

In terms of size, Shanghai Disney Resort is much more similar to the Disneyland Resort than the Walt Disney World resort. The Shanghai Disney Resort comes in at 963 acres, about twice the size of Disneyland Resort's 500 acres, or a fraction is Walt Disney World's 25,000 acres.

From the resort hotels to the parks is no more than a 20-minute walk at Shanghai Disneyland (or 5 minutes on a shuttle bus), and even less at Disneyland Resort. However, at Walt Disney World most journeys cannot be walked due to its sprawling size.

Shanghai Disney Resort only has one theme park, at Disneyland Resort the two theme parks are right next to each other, whereas everything is a monorail or bus journey away from each other at Walt Disney World.

The advantage of Shanghai Disneyland is that you can walk throughout the whole resort, you can visit any of the hotels easily, and you will spend less time traveling and more time enjoying yourself – similar to Disneyland. The disadvantage is that there are fewer things to do: no water parks, fewer hotels, and crucially fewer theme parks.

Looking at the theme parks, when counting the public areas and ride area, all of Disney's theme Magic-Kingdom-style parks are pretty comparable in size. Shanghai Disneyland itself comes in at about 105 acres in size. Disneyland Park in California and Tokyo Disneyland are both 90 acres each, Magic Kingdom is 92 acres (but 115 acres if you include the railway areas), and Disneyland Paris's park is 81 acres (100 if counting everything inside the railroad track). Shanghai Disneyland will be larger once a Zootopia expansion is finished, perhaps making it the indisputable largest.

Shanghai Disneyland is by far the biggest-'feeling' of the parks – this is probably due to huge walkways and the large hub in front of the castle.

The other thing that is different about Shanghai is the accessibility by public transportation – Shanghai Disneyland has a metro station right at its doorstep. This can't be said for Disneyland or Walt Disney World.

Also, Shanghai Disneyland and the original Disneyland Resort are both very self-contained, so if you do fancy escaping the magic, it is easy to do - unlike in Florida! For some people, this freedom is a benefit, though others prefer the Floridian immersion of the Disney magic that lets them forget about the outside world.

Pricing

Disney trips can be very pricey when you take into account all of the costs.

Hotels
At Shanghai Disney Resort you will find rooms at Toy Story Hotel vary from about ¥1,500 ($215) to ¥2,400 ($340) depending on the season and at the Shanghai Disneyland Hotel, they range from about ¥3,000 ($425) to ¥4,300 ($610).

In comparison, the Disneyland Hotel at Disneyland Resort (the cheapest onsite hotel) costs $210 to $350 per night. The grandest, the Grand Californian has room rates at $475 to $980.

At Walt Disney World, you can expect to pay $154 to $316 for a value-level room at Pop Century Resort. A room goes from $425 to $846 at the deluxe-level Beach Club Resort.

Overall here, except for some much-cheaper Value level rooms at Walt Disney World, prices seem to be on a par generally with the American hotels.

Tickets
The biggest price difference you will find is in ticket prices. A Shanghai Disneyland 1-day park ticket costs from ¥399 ($56) to ¥699 ($99).

For comparison, at Walt Disney World, a one day, one park adult ticket is $116 to $169 with tax. At Disneyland it is $104 to $154.

As we can see above, park tickets at Shanghai Disneyland are about half the price of the American parks for a single day.

Food
A bottle of water in Shanghai Disneyland is ¥10 ($1.40) with a Pepsi coming in at ¥15 ($2.15). In the US, a bottle of water or a Coke is $4 (two to three times the price).

In Shanghai, a Quick Service meal with a drink is about ¥100 ($14), whereas in the US this would cost around $16.

Snacks such as ice creams are roughly comparable in price at $4-$6 in each park.

Fastpass

Fastpass at Disneyland Resort can be done with paper tickets or (for a daily charge with an app called MaxPass) digitally. Shanghai Disneyland also has both systems but is mainly digital – the 'MaxPass' equivalent is built into the Shanghai Disney Resort app and is free.

Walt Disney World has a fully digital Fastpass+ system. With Fastpass+ you can make ride reservations on your smartphone or using in-park kiosks up to 60 days in advance, or on the day itself.

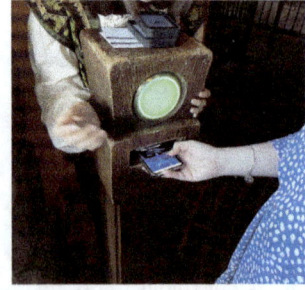

Unique Attractions and Details

Shanghai Disneyland has several unique rides and shows which cannot be found at the American Disney Parks.

In Tomorrowland you will find *TRON Lightcycle Power Run* which is a more thrilling alternative to *Space Mountain*. *Stitch Encounter* is similar to *Turtle Talk with Crush* in Epcot, and *Jet Packs* is essentially a rethemed *Dumbo* or *Astro Orbiters*.

The entirety of Toy Story Land is unique compared to the American Parks, though visitors to Disneyland Paris or Hong Kong Disneyland will have seen this area before.

Fantasyland has the unique *"Once Upon a Time Adventure"* walkthrough, *Alice in Wonderland Maze* and *Voyage to the Crystal Grotto* attractions. The other rides in this land exist in the American parks.

At Treasure Cove, you have the unique *Pirates of the Caribbean* attraction – unlike any other ride in the world. *Eye of the Storm* is also a unique stunt show, as are all the walkthrough areas here.

Finally, Adventure Isle features *Roaring Rapids* and *Camp Discovery* which cannot be found anywhere else.

Mickey Avenue, Gardens of Imagination, Treasure Cove and Adventure Isle are unique new areas of the park. Fantasyland and Tomorrowland are familiar in name but are different visually. *Enchanted Storybook Castle* is, of course, unique and the biggest Disney castle ever made. The parade and the fireworks show are also unique to the park, although Paris has now cloned Shanghai's nighttime show.

Overall, there are plenty of new things to see and do to keep Disney theme park fans busy for a full day – and longer if you plan on repeating your favorite attractions from the other parks.

…………………………………………………………………………………………………

Seasonal Events & the Future

Shanghai Disneyland offers its guests something different throughout the year, with seasonal and special events that celebrate events such as Spring, Halloween and Christmas. This section explores all of these. Then, we take a look at the future of the resort.

…………………………………………………………………………………………………

Chinese New Year
13th January to 9th February 2020

In 2020, this event was curtailed due to a global pandemic as the park shut its doors for several months on 25th January. Each year there are special limited time features during this season.

In 2020 this includes:
• The transformation of the "Twelve Friends Garden" into **the Wishing Garden** with a focus on the mosaic featuring a rat – as 2020 is the Year of the Rat in the Chinese Zodiac. Here guests can get special wishing cards to write down their wishes for this year.
• **New Year's decorations** throughout the park such as Mickey lanterns and paper decorations
• A **drumming ceremony** with Mickey and Minnie each morning
• Each evening, a **special fireworks show** is played with projections and music after *Ignite the Dream*.
• Limited time **dining and merchandise** items are also available, including Lucky Bags which feature goods that are only revealed after you have purchased them.
• The **Disney hotels** offer special activities such as lantern making, calligraphy and making masks.
• A **festival in Disneytown** with dragon dancers, performances and handmade crafts.

Spring Mini-Season
April and May

The Spring mini-season varies each year but usually includes the following:

• **Floral photo opportunities** around the park
• Disney **character 'Easter' eggs** to take photos with
• New **merchandise and dining** items

Seasonal Events and the Future

Spring Inspiration Run
18th and 19th April 2020

The Inspiration Run is a variety of races through Shanghai Disneyland, Disneytown and around Inspiration Lake with Disney characters along the route. In 2020, its third year, the resort is going with a Marvel theme for the event.

There are four main race lengths:

- Kids races – 100m dash
- 3.5K Run
- 5K Run
- 10K Run

Race participants receive a medal for each race completed and refreshments during and after their race. Special medals are available for those who complete multiple races. There is an extra chatge to participate in this event.

This event is postponed for 2020 due to a pandemic, but will return in the future.

Check the events section on www.shanghaidisneyresort.com/en/events/disney-run/ for registration.

Summer Season
July and August

The summer season at Shanghai Disneyland is all about keeping guests cool in the soaring temperatures. You may get wet!

Details vary yearly but, in the past, have included:
- A castle show – Summer Blast – featuring water jets to get the audience wet
- A pre-parade where dancers spray water at the crowds
- New merchandise and dining items

Halloween
October and early November

Halloween is one of the better developed seasons at the resort.

You can expect:
- A **Halloween Cavalcade** (mini-parade) in the evening featuring villains such as the Queen of Hearts and Maleficent, as well as Disney pals like Mickey and Duffy
- **Treasure Cove Ghost Pirates** – These pirates roam around Treasure Cove spooking guests and then perform a stunt show at Shipwreck Shore
- A **Halloween Dance Party** in Tomorrowland featuring Jack and Sally from 'A Nightmare Before Christmas'
- **Park decorations** including lanterns and pumpkins

- **Guests can dress** up in costumes
- **Trick-or-treat** spots throughout the park where Cast Members give out candy
- Halloween entertainment in **Disneytown**
- Limited time **merchandise and dining** items

All this is included in your regular park admission.

In 2019, the park had its first-ever Halloween extra-ticketed party with one-night-only entertainment and extended theme park hours. We expect this to now be a yearly feature.

Christmas

Late November to early January

Although Christmas is not part of the Chinese calendar as China is not a Christian country, Shanghai Disneyland really gets into the festive spirit.

Features of the Christmas season include:
• A **Christmas tree lighting ceremony** with music, Disney characters and a gigantic tree
• **Mickey Avenue Wonderland** where it snows on Mickey Avenue and Disney characters come out to celebrate with guests
• **Festive tunes** played by the Shanghai Disneyland Band as Disney characters appear in their Christmas costumes
• **Santa Goofy** meet-and-greet
• **Christmas jazz** and swing show
• **Decorations along Mickey Avenue** including garlands, wreaths, and festive bows
• **Disneytown** has decorations, a Santa meet-and-greet, Christmas carolers and even its own tree-lighting ceremony
• Limited time **merchandise and dining** items

All this is included in your regular park admission.

The Future

New Zootopia Land

Shanghai Disneyland is set to expand with a new area themed around the Zootopia movie – we expect this to open in 2021 or 2022 if everything goes to plan, although Disney has not revealed an opening date at the moment.

No details have been given by Disney except for this concept art. The official information tells us that "the eighth themed land will be an immersive mammal metropolis that brings a variety of fan-favorite Zootopia citizens to life. This exciting expansion will allow guests to experience signature key offerings like new "Zootopia"-themed merchandise, entertainment and creatively curated

cuisine. The land will also feature a new major attraction – one that's sure to create unforgettable guest memories with its innovative technology and immersive storytelling."

Resort Expansion

Rumors tell us that, in the long-term, Disney's plan is to have three theme parks at the Shanghai Disney Resort with several more hotels too. The resort is only 4 years old so only time will tell what is to come.

A Special Thanks

Thank you very much for reading our travel guide. We hope this book has made a big difference to your trip to the Shanghai Disney Resort, and that you have found some tips that will save you time, money and hassle! Remember to take this guide with you when you are visiting the resort. This guide is also available in a printed format.

If you have any feedback about any element of the guide, or have noticed changes in the parks that differ from what is in the book, do let us know by sending us a message. To contact us, visit our website at www.independentguidebooks.com.

If you enjoyed the guide, we would love for you to leave a review on Amazon or wherever you have purchased this guide. Your reviews make a huge difference in helping other people find this guide. Thank you.

Have a magical time!

If you have enjoyed this guide, other travel guides in this series include:
- The Independent Guide to Walt Disney World
- The Independent Guide to Tokyo Disney Resort
- The Independent Guide to Disneyland Paris
- The Independent Guide to Universal Orlando
- The Independent Guide to Universal Studios Hollywood
- The Independent Guide to Disneyland
- The Independent Guide to Hong Kong
- The Independent Guide to Tokyo
- The Independent Guide to Dubai
- The Independent Guide to Paris
- The Independent Guide to London
- The Independent Guide to New York City

Coming later in 2020 are new guides to Hong Kong Disneyland and Universal Studios Japan too.

Photo credits:

The following photos in this guide have been used from Flickr (unless otherwise stated) under a Creative Commons license. Thank you to: Pirates – Jeremy Thompson;

Some images are copyright The Walt Disney Company and Shanghai Disney Resort.

Shanghai Disneyland Map

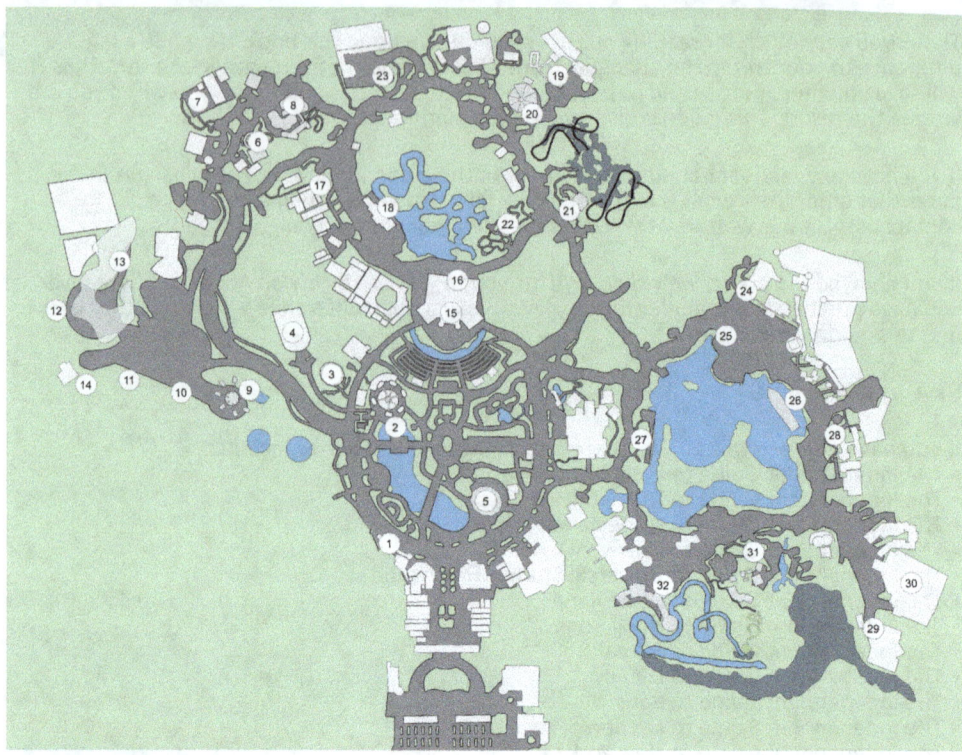

MICKEY AVENUE
1 - Mickey's Film Festival

GARDENS OF IMAGINATION
2 - Dumbo the Flying Elephant
3 - Meet Mickey Tent
4 - Marvel Universe
5 - Fantasia Carousel

DISNEY PIXAR TOY STORY LAND
6 - Slinky Dog Spin
7 - Rex's Racer
8 - Woody's Roundup

TOMORROWLAND
9 - Jet Packs
10 - Stitch Encounter
11 - Buzz Lightyear Planet Rescue
12 - TRON Realm
13 - TRON Lightcycle Power Run
14 - Star Wars Launch Bay

FANTASYLAND
15 - Enchanted Storybook Castle
16 - "Once Upon a Time Adventure"
17 - Peter Pan's Flight
18 - Voyage to the Crystal Grotto
19 - The Many Adventures of Winnie the Pooh
20 - Hunny Pot Spin
21 - Seven Dwarfs Mine Train
22 - Alice in Wonderland Maze
23 - FROZEN: A Sing-Along Celebration

TREASURE COVE
24 - Pirates of the Caribbean: Battle for the Sunken Treasure
25 - Shipwreck Shore
26 - Siren's Revenge
27 - Explorer Canoes
28 - Eye of the Storm - Captain Jack's Stunt Spectacular

ADVENTURE ISLE
29 - Soaring Over the Horizon
30 - Storyhouse Stage
31 - Camp Discovery including Challenge Trails
32 - Roaring Rapids

www.ingramcontent.com/pod-product-compliance
Lightning Source LLC
LaVergne TN
LVHW021945060526
838200LV00042B/1925